BABIES
An Unsentimental Anthology

At first the infant,
Mewling and puking in his nurse's arms.

SHAKESPEARE *As You Like It*, 1599,
Act II, Sc. vii.

BABIES

An Unsentimental Anthology

Iona and Peter Opie

With drawings by Bob Graham

JOHN MURRAY

First published in 1990
by John Murray (Publishers) Ltd
50 Albemarle Street, London W1X 4BD

British Library Cataloguing in Publication Data
Opie, Iona 1923–
Babies: an unsentimental anthology.
1. Babies
I. Title II. Opie, Peter 1918–1982
305.232

ISBN 0-7195-4855-1

Photoset by Rowland Phototypesetting Ltd
Bury St Edmunds, Suffolk
Printed by Butler and Tanner Ltd
Frome and London

Contents

Foreword

'Love needs no teaching', they say, but we are now so remote from our instincts that sometimes we fumble for them in vain. A young couple meeting their first baby for the first time, and hoping that biology will guide them towards successful parenthood, may be disoriented by a mass of preconceived notions and literary conceptions, pieced together from books and pictures and the sentiments of older people, and feel, to their disappointment, that the newly delivered child is not quite as advertised. Why is it not angelically pink-and-white; why is it not smiling at them? These starry expectations are as unreal and dangerous as the love stories in women's magazines.

When I was handed my first baby I was simply not interested in him. He was like a tiny mandarin, his yellow skin blotched with purple. They showed me how to get his wind up by pressing on his tummy, and then took him away again – so I went on reading. Peter and I had not intended to be parents so soon, but, finding ourselves with a new subject to study, we enrolled with Dr Grantly Dick Read and became exponents of natural childbirth. We conscientiously bought the recommended equipment. As for the baby itself, we hardly thought about it. Probably we assumed that we would like it, and that it would like us.

Peter was an only child, and I was the younger of two. Babies had never intruded upon our lives, nor were there any amongst our acquaintance. At most, we had encountered the chubby babies in advertisements for baby food, the cherubic babies on sheets of embossed Victorian scraps, the cute finger-in-mouth babies drawn by Mabel Lucie Attwell, and the babies in some Victorian poems supposed to be suitable for children to learn by heart – George MacDonald's 'Where did you come from, baby dear?', for instance. We had overheard women in the street, as they leaned over prams and poked or tickled the occupants into sociability, asking embarrassing, unanswerable questions like '*Who*'s a big boy then? Isn't he just like his Daddy?', and finishing with a fervent '*Bless* his little cotton socks'; and we had listened to women at tea parties, enthusing about an expected event as they knitted in pink and blue.

Even if we, as children, rejected babies as unworthy of notice (and I, as a small girl, rejected baby dolls in favour of teddy bears), we both received a lasting impression that babies were considered adorable, and that it was the accepted thing to love and admire them. What we did not know was that this tide of adulation was already ebbing; it had been in full flood in the late Victorian era, when, in a curious parallel to the medieval worship of the Madonna and Child, the purity of women and the perfection of babyhood were affirmed with an almost religious intensity. Among the middle and upper classes, especially, a strength of sentiment existed which now seems excessive, and which spilt over into sentimentality. This may have been due, in part, to German *Sensibilität*. Sentimental German prints, greetings cards,

sweet-faced dolls, nursery ornaments, scraps, and illustrated children's books poured on to the English market in the late nineteenth century, to satisfy a yearning for cosy family scenes, winsome babies, fluffy kittens and roguish puppies which the two countries seemed to share.

It comes as a shock, after all this baby worship, to learn that there were periods in history when babies were not thought of as particularly precious. In the ancient world, for economic and patriarchal reasons, unwanted children were left in frequented places such as the market square to be adopted; in later centuries they would be put into an orphanage. Realism and common sense prevailed. In the twelfth century Heloise refused to marry the scholar Peter Abelard, father of her son, for, she said, 'How can the Study of Divinity and Philosophy comport with the Cries of Children?' (One is reminded of Robert Graves at World's End Cottage, in the 1920s, acquiring the 'faculty of working through constant interruptions . . . recognising the principal varieties of babies' screams – hunger, indigestion, wetness, pins, boredom, wanting to be played with – and learning to disregard all but the more important ones.') In the early eighteenth century Moll Flanders, in Defoe's story, congratulated herself that when her young husband died 'My two children were indeed taken happily off of my hands, by my husband's father and mother'. *The Statistical Account of Scotland*, 1794, tells us that an arrangement called *hand-fasting* was customary between young people who thought they might like to get married. They lived together for a year, on approval, and parted if the relationship had not proved happy. 'The fruit of the connexion (if there were any),' adds the *Account*, 'was always attached to the dis-

affected person.' In other words, the one who defaulted had to take the baby, which was looked upon as a liability.

Women in poorer districts would not, indeed, have thought of their babies in at all the same terms as the adoring (or dutiful) mothers who spent with their darlings only an hour or so a day. Well-read mothers could think of their babies as 'bits of star-dust blown from the hand of God', or 'living jewels dropped unstained from heaven'; they were able to believe, with Wordsworth, that 'trailing clouds of glory do we come, From God, who is our home', and even agree with Martin F. Tupper that 'A babe in the house is a well-spring of pleasure'. They could sing at a candle-lit piano:

> When the birds are waking baby's laugh is heard,
> O'er the house her little feet they patter;
> Then her mamma calling, sweeter than a bird
> All about the house you hear her chatter.
> Little mischief, you,
> Mamma's precious treasure,
> Little mischief, you,
> Papa's hope and pearl;

Little mischief, you,
  Filling life with pleasure,
Mamma's and papa's baby girl.

Poets and song-writers might wax lyrical about babyhood in that highly emotional era, and between the wars much playful verse about babies and children was published; but a less poetic view is taken by those who have the care of their own children twenty-four hours a day. They notice, among the much-publicized charms, some less appealing characteristics. Babies and toddlers are well fitted for trying the patience of a saint; they are not so well qualified as intellectual companions. And the situation is exacerbated when the child-minder would greatly prefer to be doing something else, even if it is only holding a reasonable conversation with another adult. We have sympathy with the erstwhile young executive who, immured with her cherished one-year-old, cried out 'I'm so bored. We've played peek-a-boo round the sofa for hours, and there's nothing left to do.' And with the eighteen-year-old whose husband left her alone with their baby every night, to meet his friends at the pub. And with the young mother in Kensington Gardens whom we overheard screaming at her baby, as he sat round-eyed in his pram, 'You've ruined my life! You don't seem to realize!'

Peter and I forgave our first baby for being a baby as soon as he was able to appreciate nursery rhymes. He co-operated most willingly as we tested their pleasing rhythms; and when we sat at the Pembroke table making notes on their histories, he sat placidly within the bars below, playing with our toes. It was not until the second and third babies arrived that the frustrations and difficulties of parenthood became fully apparent, for as the old rhyme has it,

> With one you may run,
> With two you may go,
> But with three you mun bide where you be.

We were not able to live at the slow, pastoral pace which makes bearable the tending of babies and toddlers; and, even though we had intermittent help, it proved difficult to write books in the same house as small children. Peter, especially, felt entirely besieged in his upstairs study; and he stayed there all day, except for exasperated (and exasperating) forays to enquire why there was so much noise ('Can't it be stopped?'). Life seemed more chaotic than it need be, and for a while we wondered whether we were the wrong kind of parents or, alternatively, whether we had the wrong kind of children. We spent a large proportion of our nights trying to rock the most wakeful of the infants to sleep in the currently fashionable Treasure Cot, which was dispiritingly hygienic and would not rock; and a large part of our days was devoted to servicing the children's somewhat erratic alimentary systems. Why had nobody told us about the noise, and the mess?

As we read widely in search of the histories of nursery rhymes, we noticed passages pointing out, with a kind of resigned and humorous affection, the less glamorous aspects of rearing a family. We seized on them with glee, and when we gazed fondly at a serenely sleeping face that minutes before had been distorted by demonic fury we murmured:

> Now God be praised, the battle's by,
> And sleep has won at last.[1]

We started to make notes, and to line up a rogues' gallery of babies. Here was the relentless howler ('A Serenade', p. 34; Judge Parry, p. 88); the regrettably natural young animal, 'wet at both ends' ('Nurse's Song', p. 14); the ugly-wug (Queen Victoria, p. 45; George du Maurier, p. 89); and the frightening precocity (Heraclês, p. 3; 'Johnnie in the Cradle', p. 100). Here were babies in the rôles of dictator (*Gulliver's Travels*, p. 11; C. M. Yonge, p. 73); of wrecker ('A Parental Ode', p. 31; 'Willie Winkie', p. 37); of encumbrance (Surtees, p. 38; Seldon Truss, p. 111); and of financial liability (*Poor Robin's Almanack*, p. 10; 'Good-by Bill', p. 99).

Only once is a baby's opinion heard (in 'Who took me from my nice warm cot?', p. 91), but disgruntled siblings have their say ('Antonia', p. 110; Dirk Bogarde, p. 128), and it becomes clear that children in general do not always see the appeal of tiny mites (E. Nesbit, p. 93; *Just-William*, p. 104; school rhymes, pp. 94–6).

As for the adults, they appear in the guise of embarrassed bachelors (Jerome K. Jerome, p. 85; Beverley Nichols, p. 115); weary mothers (*Amantium Irae*, p. 6; 'O can ye sew

[1] This became traditional in the family and, as is usual with traditional lore, its source was forgotten. In spite of a long search I have been unable to find the author.

cushions?', p. 23); nervous, or loftily aloof, fathers ('The Kid', p. 77, and *Sense and Sensibility*, p. 24); philosophers who see babyhood as an opportunity for improving the human race (*Utopia*, p. 5; *Brave New World*, p. 107); a film star who regards a baby only as a rival (W. C. Fields, p. 106); an irascible old gentleman spluttering with annoyance over the 'nasty little ugly babies in the streets' ('Perambulators and Pedestrians', p. 42); and a nursemaid getting her own back on her little charges ('Invaluable Hints', p. 40).

In this book devoted parents will find their less admissible feelings set out in prose and verse by authors who have looked on babies with clear eyes over the past two thousand years. They will recognize that strange syndrome in which the baby who tugs at your heartstrings at 10 a.m. becomes the monster you could murder (if it were not for the law) at noon. The only antidotes are laughter and the experience of others; and so, in the tranquillity of grandmotherhood, I have finally assembled the book we ourselves needed in the 1940s, hoping it will amuse the young parents of the present day. I wish them good luck, and greet them with the phrase that prefaced the publications of the ancients:

'Χαὶϱετε' – 'Be happy!'

IONA OPIE

BABIES
An Unsentimental Anthology

When Isaac prayed that God would lift the twenty-year curse of barrenness from Rebekah, she at once conceived twins. Soon they began struggling with each other in her womb, so violently that she longed for death; but God reassured Rebekah . . . Whenever Rebekah passed a Canaanite shrine during her pregnancy, Esau struggled to get out; whenever she passed a house of righteous prayer, Jacob did likewise. For he had addressed Esau in the womb: 'The world of flesh, my brother, is not the world of spirit. Here is eating and drinking, marriage and procreation; there none of these are found. Let us divide the worlds between us. Take which you prefer!' Esau hastily chose the world of flesh.

Hebrew Myths: The Book of Genesis, Robert Graves and Raphael Patai, 1963, ch. 38

The greatest of all the Heroes was Heraclês. He was the son of Zeus and Alcmena, princess of Thebes, and there was great excitement over his birth. Hera was jealous and angry; and as soon as he was born, with his twin-brother Iphiclês, she sent two large serpents into the chamber, to kill the babies. But Heraclês lifted up his head, and clutched the throats of the two serpents, and held them writhing until their lives were throttled out of them. Up jumped his mother, and ran to help, and all the women shrieked out, 'He's dead!' In came the men, clad in full armour, in came Prince Amphitryon, holding a drawn sword in his hand. When he saw the baby Heraclês, with a serpent hanging limp from each hand, he cried out, 'Who told me the baby was dead? It is the serpents that are dead!'

W. H. D. ROUSE *Gods, Heroes and Men of Ancient Greece*, pt. 2

I should like to tell you some of the odd things I noticed during my stay on the Moon . . . as they have never even heard of women up there, the men just marry other men, and these other men have the babies . . . When a man is pregnant, he carries the child not in his stomach but in the calf of his leg, which grows extremely fat on these occasions. In due course they do a Caesarean, and the baby is taken out dead; but it is then brought to life by being placed in a high wind with its mouth open . . . Even more surprising is the method of propagating what are known as Tree-Men. This how it is done: you cut off the father's right testicle and plant it in the ground, where it grows into a large fleshy tree rather like a phallus, except that it has leaves and branches and bears fruit in the form of acorns, which are about eighteen inches long. When the fruit is ripe, it is picked and the babies inside are hatched out . . . They [the men] use their stomachs as handbags for carrying things around in, for they can open and shut them at will. If you look inside one, there is nothing to be seen in the way of digestive organs, but the whole interior is lined with fur so that it can also be used as a centrally-heated pram for babies in cold weather.

LUCIAN OF SAMOSATA (born *c.* AD 120)
True History, trans. Paul Turner, 1958, pt. I

There are pearls to be found on the beaches, diamonds and garnets on certain types of rock – but they never bother to look for them. However, if they happen to come across one, they pick it up and polish it for some toddler to wear. At first, children are terribly proud of such jewellery – until they're old enough to register that it's only worn in the nursery. Then, without any prompting from their parents, but purely as a matter of self-respect, they give it up – just as our children grow out of things like dolls, and conkers, and lucky charms. This curious convention is liable to cause some equally curious reactions, as I realised most vividly in the case of the Flatulentine diplomats . . . They wore cloth of gold, with great gold chains round their necks, gold ear-rings dangling from their ears, and gold rings on their fingers. Their very hats were festooned with glittering ropes of pearls and other jewels . . . you should have seen the faces of the older children, who'd grown out of things like pearls and jewels, when they saw the ones on the envoys' hats. They kept nudging their mothers and whispering: 'I say, Mother, just look at that great baby! Fancy wearing jewellery at his age!'

THOMAS MORE *Utopia*, trans. Paul Turner, 1516, Book II

In going to my naked bed, as one that would have slept,
I heard a wife sing to her child, that long before had wept.
She sighed sore, and sang full sweet, to bring the child to
rest,
That would not cease, but cried still in sucking at her
breast.
She was full weary of her watch and grieved with her child,
She rocked it, and rated it, till that on her it smiled.
Then did she say, 'Now have I found this proverb true to
prove:
The falling out of faithful friends, renewing is of love.'

RICHARD EDWARDES *Amantium Irae*, 1580

A father now who sees his infant born,
What joy, oh, what delight! At once he wraps
The babe in napkins and in swaddling-clothes;
And like a pair of scales he loads him up
And hangs about his neck a thousand things –
Wolves' teeth and figs, half-moons and coral too,
Toy pigs and badgers, till the infant looks
Just like the man who hawks around old clothes.
He hires a nurse and prattles baby talk,
And has no eye for any other thing,
'How is my little love, my little pet?
Your papa loves you well, you are his joy,
Your mamma's only treasure', there he sits
List'ning amazed to 'cacca' and 'pappa.'
While in his lap, the baby wets him through.

GIAMBATTISTA BASILE *The Pentamerone*, 1634,
Day III, Eclogue. The setting is Naples.

The Tythe. To the Bride

If nine times you your Bride-groome kisse;
The tenth you know the Parson's is.
Pay then your Tythe; and doing thus,
Prove in your Bride-bed numerous.
If children you have ten, Sir John
Won't for his tenth part ask you one.

HERRICK *Hesperides*, 1648

25 May. *Lords day* . . . To church and heard a good sermon of Mr Woodcockes at our church. Only, in his later prayer for a woman in childbed, he prayed that God would deliver her from the hereditary curse of childebearing, which seemed a pretty strange expression.

PEPYS *Diary*, 1662

8 February. Creede and I and Captain Ferrers to the parke – and there walked finely, seeing people slide – we talking all the while and Captain Ferrers telling me, among other Court passages – how about a month ago, at a Ball at Court, a child was dropped by one of the ladies in dancing; but nobody knew who, it being taken up by somebody in their handkercher. The next morning all the Ladies of Honour appeared early at Court for their vindication, so that nobody could tell whose this mischance should be. But it seems Mrs Wells fell sick that afternoon and hath disappeared ever since, so that it is concluded it was her.[1]

17 February. Coming home, I brought Mr Pickering as far as the Temple; who tells me the story is very [true] of a child being dropped at the Ball at Court; and that the King had it in his closet a week after, and did dissect it; and making great sport of it, said that in his opinion it must have been a month and three houres old and that whatever others think, he had the greatest loss (it being a boy, as he says), that had lost a subject by the business.

Ibid. 1663

[1]Winifred Wells was a Maid of Honour to the Queen. The King was said to have been the father.

February

By this month it doth appear
That this same it is Leap-year,
Which is the cause as some men tell,
Makes womens bellies so to swell;
For 'tis a thing well worth our heeding,
Women such years are always breeding:
And then by that means you know,
Great charges doe to Husbands grow
For a Nurse the Child to dandle,
Sugar sops, spic'd pots, and candle,
A Groaning Chair, and eke a Cradle,
And ten times more then he is able;
Blanckets of a several scantling
Therein for to wrap the Bantling:
Sweet meats from Comfitmakers trade,
When the Child's a Christian made.
With many other things beside,
Against that time he must provide.
Pin-cushions and such other knacks,
A Child-bed woman always lacks.
Candles, Grewels, costly jellies,
To fill again their wambling bellies.
By all which things the case is clear,
That chargeable is a Leap-year.

Poor Robin's Almanack, 1676

scantling, size *Bantling*, small child *Comfitmakers*, sweet-makers

When dinner was almost done, the nurse came in with a child of a year old in her arms, who immediately spied me, and began a squall that you might have heard from London Bridge to Chelsea, after the usual oratory of infants, to get me for a plaything. The mother out of pure indulgence took me up, and put me towards the child, who presently seized me by the middle, and got my head into his mouth, where I roared so loud that the urchin was frightened and let me drop, and I should infallibly have broken my neck if the mother had not held her apron under me. The nurse to quiet her babe made use of a rattle, which was a kind of hollow vessel filled with great stones, and fastened by a cable to the child's waist; but all in vain, so that she was forced to apply the last remedy by giving it suck. I must confess no object ever disgusted me so much as the sight of her monstrous breast, which I cannot tell what to compare with, so as to give the curious reader an idea of its bulk, shape, and colour . . . This made me reflect upon the fair skins of our English ladies, who appear so beautiful to us, only because they are of our own size, and their defects not to be seen but through a magnifying-glass, where we find by experiment that the smoothest and whitest skins look rough and coarse, and ill-coloured.

JONATHAN SWIFT *Gulliver's Travels*, 1726, pt. 2,
'A Voyage to Brobdingnag', ch. 2

A Modest Proposal for preventing the Children of poor People from being a Burthen to their Parents or Country, and for making them Beneficial to the Publick

The number of Souls in this Kingdom [Ireland] being usually reckoned one Million and a half, Of these I calculate there may be about two hundred thousand Couple whose Wives are Breeders; from which number I subtract thirty Thousand Couples, who are able to maintain their own Children, although I apprehend there cannot be so many, under the present Distresses of the Kingdom; but this being granted, there will remain an hundred and seventy thousand Breeders. I again Subtract fifty Thousand, for those Women who miscarry, or whose Children die by accident, or disease within the Year. There only remain an hundred and twenty thousand Children of poor Parents annually born: The question therefore is, How this number shall be reared, and provided for, which . . . is utterly impossible by all the Methods hitherto proposed; for we can neither employ them in Handicraft or Agriculture; we neither build, (I mean in the Country) nor cultivate Land: They can very seldom pick up a Livelyhood by Stealing till they arrive at six years Old; except where they are of towardly parts . . .

I have been assured by a very knowing American of my acquaintance in London, that a young healthy Child well Nursed is at a year Old a most delicious nourishing and wholesome Food, whether Stewed, Roasted, Baked, or Boiled, and I make no doubt that it will equally serve in a Fricasie, or a Ragoust. I do therefore humbly offer it to publick consideration, that of the Hundred and twenty thousand Children, already computed, twenty thousand may be reserved for Breed, whereof only one fourth part to be Males; which is more than we allow to Sheep, black Cattle, or Swine, and my Reason is, that these Children are seldom the Fruits of Marriage, a Circumstance not much regarded by our Savages, therefore, one Male will be sufficient to serve four Females. That the remaining Hundred thousand may at a year Old be offered in Sale to the Persons of Quality and Fortune, through the Kingdom, always advising the Mother to let them Suck plentifully in the last Month, so as to render them Plump, and Fat for a good Table . . .

I grant this food will be somewhat dear, and therefore very proper for Landlords, who, as they have already devoured most of the Parents seem to have the Best Title to the Children . . . I believe no Gentleman would repine to give Ten Shillings for the Carcass of a good fat Child, which . . . will make four Dishes of excellent Nutritive Meat, when he hath only some particular Friend, or his own Family to dine with him. Thus the Squire will learn to be a good Landlord, and grow popular among his Tenants, the Mother will have Eight Shillings neat profit, and be fit for Work till she produces another Child.

JONATHAN SWIFT *A Modest Proposal*, 1729

The Nurse's Song

Hey! my kitten, a kitten,
Hey! my kitten, a deary;
Such a sweet pet as this
Is neither far nor neary:
Here we go up, up, up;
Here we go down, down, downy;
Here we go backwards and forwards,
And here we round, round, roundy.

Chicky, cockow, my lily cock;
See, see, sic a downy;
Gallop a trot, trot, trot,
And hey for Dublin towny.
This pig went to market;
Squeak, mouse, mouse, mousy;
Shoe, shoe, shoe the wild colt,
And hear thy own doll dousy.

Where was a jewel and pet?
Where was a sugar and spicy?
Hush a baba in a cradle,
And we'll go abroad in a tricy.
Did-a papa torment it?
Did-e vex his own baby? did-e?
Hush a baby in a bosie
Take ous own sucky: did-e?

Good-morrow, a pudding is broke;
Slavers a thread o' crystal,
Now the sweet posset comes up;
Who said my child was piss'd all?
Come water my chickens, come clock.
Leave off, or he'll crawl you, he'll crawl you;
Come, gie me your hand, and I'll beat him:
Wha was it vex'd my baby?

Where was a laugh and a craw;
Where was, was, was a giggling honey?
Goody, good child shall be fed,
But naughty child shall get nony.
Get ye gone, raw-head and bloody bones,
Here is a child that won't fear ye.
Come pissy, pissy, my jewel,
And ik, ik, ay, my deary.

Allan Ramsay's *Tea-Table Miscellany*, IV, 1740

The cares and disquietudes of the marriage state, quoth Mrs Wadman, are very great. I suppose so – said my uncle Toby: and therefore when a person, continued Mrs Wadman, is so much at his ease as you are – so happy, Captain Shandy, in yourself, your friends and your amusements – I wonder, what reasons can incline you to the state –

– They are written, quoth my uncle Toby, in the Common-Prayer Book.

Thus far my uncle Toby went on warily, and kept within his depth, leaving Mrs Wadman to sail upon the gulph as she pleased.

– As for children – said Mrs Wadman – though a principal end perhaps of the institution, and the natural wish, I suppose, of every parent – yet do not we all find, they are certain sorrows, and very uncertain comforts? and what is there, dear sir, to pay one for the heart-aches – what compensation for the many tender and disquieting apprehensions of a suffering and defenceless mother who brings them into life? I declare, said my uncle Toby, smit with pity, I know of none; unless it be the pleasure which it has pleased God –

A fiddlestick! quoth she.

LAURENCE STERNE *Tristram Shandy*, IX, 1767

BOSWELL. 'If, Sir, you were shut up in a castle, and a new-born child with you, what would you do?' JOHNSON. 'Why, Sir, I should not much like my company.'

Boswell's Life of Johnson, 26 October 1769

O that I had ne'er been married,
I wad nevir had nae care,
Now I've gotten wife and bairns
An' they cry 'crowdie' evermair.

Ance crowdie, twice crowdie,
Three times crowdie in a day:
Gin ye crowdie ony mair
Ye'll crowdie a' my meal away!

Old Scottish popular song

crowdie, oatmeal gruel

Last day when I dined at Beauclerk's, Langton said to me, 'Shall we petition to have the young gentleman brought in?' (I am now writing on Saturday the 27 at Bath.) He meant Beauclerk's son, a child about two year old. Thinking this affectation in Langton, willing to check him and to indulge the spirit of contradiction, especially as I had heard Beauclerk satirize Langton's affectation of this sort and his plaguing people with his own children, I answered, 'I'll petition for no such thing. I don't like other people's children. I think it pretty well if a man can bear his own.' Here I affected more roughness than I always possess, though in general it is certainly true that I do not like to have young children brought in, as I am disgusted with them, and dislike being in a manner forced to pay foolish compliments to their parents. Dr Johnson said last night at Thrale's that I was right. He maintained too that there were many people who had no concern about their children, who, from being engaged in business, or from their course of life in whatever way, seldom saw their children. '*I*,' said he,' should not have had much fondness for a child of my own.' 'Nay,' said Mrs Thrale. 'At least,' said he, 'I never wished to have a child.'

JAMES BOSWELL *Journal*, 11 April 1776

Doctor Collier used to say speaking of Parental Affection that one loved one's Children in Anticipation, one hopes they will one day become useful, estimable, & amiable Beings – one cannot love lumps of Flesh continued he, and they are nothing better during Infancy.

MRS THRALE *Diary*, 1777

The Birth and Christening of Little Cunny

The sun has loos'd his weary team,
And turn'd his steeds a-grazing;
Ten fathoms deep in Neptune's stream
His Thetis was embracing.
The stars they tripped in the firmament,
Like milk-maids on a May-day,
Or country lasses a-mumming sent,
Or school-boys on a play-day.

Apace came on the grey-ey'd morn,
The herds in fields were lowing;
And 'mongst the poultry in the barn,
The ploughman's cock sat crowing:
When Roger, dreaming of golden joys,
Was wak'd by a bawling rout, sir:
For Cissy told him he needs must rise,
His Juggy was crying out, sir.

Not half so quickly the cups go round,
At the tapping a good ale firkin,
As Roger hosen and shoon had found,
And button'd his leathern jerkin:
Grey mare was saddled with wond'rous speed,
With pillion on buttock right, sir;
And thus he to an old midwife rode,
To bring the poor kid to light, sir.

Up, up, dear mother, then Roger cries,
The fruit of my labour's now come;
In Juggy's belly it sprawling lies,
And cannot get out till you come.
I'll help it, cries the old hag, ne'er doubt,
Thy Jug shall be well again, boy;
I'll get the urchin as safely out,
As ever it did get in, boy.

The mare now bustles with all her feet,
No whipping or spurs were wanting;
At last into the good house they get,
And mew soon cried the bantling.
A female chit so small was born,
They put it into a flaggon,
And must be christen'd that very morn,
For fear it should die a Pagan.

Now Roger struts about the hall,
As great as the Prince of Condé:
The midwife cries, her parts are small,
But they will grow larger one day;
What though her thighs and legs lie close,
And little as any spider,
They will, when up to her teens she grows,
By the grace of the Lord, lie wider.

And now the merry spic'd bowls went round,
The gossips were void of shame too;
In butter'd ale the priest half drown'd
Demands the infant's name too.
Some call'd it Phill, some Florida,
But Kate was allow'd the best hint,
For she would have it Cunicula,
'Cause there was a pretty jest in't.

Thus Cunny of Winchester was known,
And famous in Kent and Dover,
And highly rated in London town,
And courted the kingdom over.
The charms of Cunny, by sea and land,
Subdues each human creature,
And will our stubborn hearts command,
Whilst there is a man in nature.

The Convivial Songster, 1782

'Our childer, I can never dout it,
Will comely as their mither be;
And in wit and prudence surelie
Thay will coppie after me.

Sae our race will bear perfection
Baith in bodie and in saul;
Surlie a mair happy marriage
To man's lot docht never fall.'

Sae the wicht fou fondlie dremit –
Alack the issue was far ither!
The bairns were ugly as their daddie,
And thay were foolish as their mither.

Select Scottish Ballads, J. Pinkerton, II, 1783

wicht, fellow

Nursing Song

O can ye sew cushions,
And can ye sew sheets,
And can ye sing bal-lu-loo
When the bairn greets?

And hee and baw birdie
And hee and baw lamb,
And hee and baw birdie,
My bonnie wee lamb.

Hee O wee O,
What would I do wi' you?
Black's the life
That I lead wi' you.

Monny o' you,
Little for to gie you,
Hee O wee O,
What would I do wi' you?

Johnson's *Musical Museum*, V, 1797

Mr Palmer maintained the common, but unfatherly opinion among his sex, of all infants being alike; and although she could plainly perceive at different times, the most striking resemblance between this baby and every one of his relations on both sides, there was no convincing his father of it; no persuading him to believe that it was not exactly like every other baby of the same age; nor could he even be brought to acknowledge the simple proposition of its being the finest child in the world.

JANE AUSTEN *Sense and Sensibility*, 1811, II, ch. 14

Needles and pins, needles and pins,
When a man marries his trouble begins;
Blankets and sheets, blankets and sheets,
When a man marries he's bothered wi' geits
[children]

Traditional

Thomas Hills Everitt

This prodigious child, an extraordinary instance of the sudden and rapid increase of the human body, was born on the 7th of February 1779. His father, a mould-paper mark-maker, conducted the paper-mills by the side of Enfield Marsh, and was about thirty-six years of age; the mother was forty-two, but neither of the parents was remarkable for either size or stature. Thomas was their fifth child, and the eldest of the three living in 1780 was twelve years old, and rather small of his age; but the paternal grandfather was of a size larger than ordinary. They had another son of uncommon size, who died of the measles of January 1774, at the age of fifteen months.

Thomas was not remarkably large when born, but began,

when six weeks old, to grow apace, and attained a most extraordinary size. At the age of nine months and two weeks, his dimensions were taken by Mr Sherwen, an ingenious surgeon residing at Enfield, and compared with those of a lusty boy seven years old. The result was as follows:–

	Dimensions of the child. Inches	Of the boy Inches
Girth round the wrist	6¾	4¾
Ditto above the elbow	8½	6¼
Ditto of the leg near the ancle	9¾	6¼
Ditto of the calf of the leg	12	9
Ditto round the thigh	18	12¾
Ditto round the small of the back	24	22
Ditto under the arm-pits and across the breast	22¾	24

Mr Sherwen who, in November, 1779, transmitted the above account to Mr Planta, secretary of the Royal Society, added, that he should have been glad to have given the solid contents of animal substance, but was prevented by the vulgar prejudice entertained by the mother against weighing children. He could therefore only say that, when she exposed to view his legs, thighs, and broad back, it was impossible to be impressed with any other idea than that of seeing a young giant. His weight was, however, guessed at nine stone, and his height at this period was three feet one inch and a quarter.

The child was soon afterwards conveyed to the house of a relation in Great Turnstile, Holborn; but the confined situation had such an effect on his health, that it was found necessary to carry him back to his native air. His extraordinary size tempted his parents to remove him again to the metropolis, and to exhibit him to the public. His dimensions, as stated in the handbills distributed at the place of exhibition, and under a picture of Mrs Everitt and her son, published in January 1780 . . . were taken when he was eleven months old. His height was then three feet three inches; his girth round the breast, two feet six inches; the loins, three feet one inch; the thigh, one foot ten inches; the leg, one foot two inches; the arm, eleven inches and a half; the wrist, nine inches.

He was well-proportioned all over, and subsisted entirely on the breast. His countenance was comely, but had rather more expression than is usual at his age, and was exceedingly pleasing, from his being uncommonly good-tempered. He had very fine hair, pure skin, free from any blemish, was extremely lively, and had a bright clear eye. His head was rather smaller in proportion than his other parts. From these circumstances Mr Sherwen ventured to prognosticate that he was as likely to arrive at maturity, accidental diseases excepted, as any child he ever saw. This opinion might, undoubtedly, have been well founded, notwithstanding the child's death; which took place about the middle of 1780, before he had attained the age of eighteen months.

Wonderful Characters, Henry Wilson, III, 1821

Baby, baby, naughty baby,
Hush, you squalling thing, I say.
Peace this moment, peace, or maybe
Bonaparte will pass this way.

Baby, baby, he's a giant,
Tall and black as Rouen steeple,
And he breakfasts, dines, rely on't,
Every day on naughty people.

Baby, baby, if he hears you,
As he gallops past the house,
Limb from limb at once he'll tear you,
Just as pussy tears a mouse.

And he'll beat you, beat you, beat you,
And he'll beat you all to pap,
And he'll eat you, eat you, eat you,
Every morsel snap, snap, snap.

Traditional

A Parental Ode to my Son, Aged Three Years and Five Months

Thou happy, happy elf!
(But stop – first let me kiss away that tear)
Thou tiny image of myself!
(My love, he's poking peas into his ear!)
Thou merry, laughing sprite!
With spirits feather-light,
Untouched by sorrow and unsoiled by sin –
(Good heavens, the child is swallowing a pin!)

Thou tricksy Puck!
With antic toys so funnily bestuck,
Light as the singing bird that wings the air –
(The door! the door! he'll tumble down the stair!)
Thou darling of thy sire!
(Why, Jane, he'll set his pinafore a-fire!)
Thou imp of mirth and joy!
In love's dear chain so strong and bright a link,
Thou idol of thy parents – (Drat the boy!
There goes my ink!)

Thou cherub! – but of earth;
Fit playfellow for Fays, by moonlight pale,
In harmless sport and mirth,
(That dog will bite him if he pulls its tail!)
Thou human humming-bee, extracting honey
From every blossom in the world that blows,
Singing in Youth's Elysium ever sunny –
(Another tumble! – that's his precious nose!)

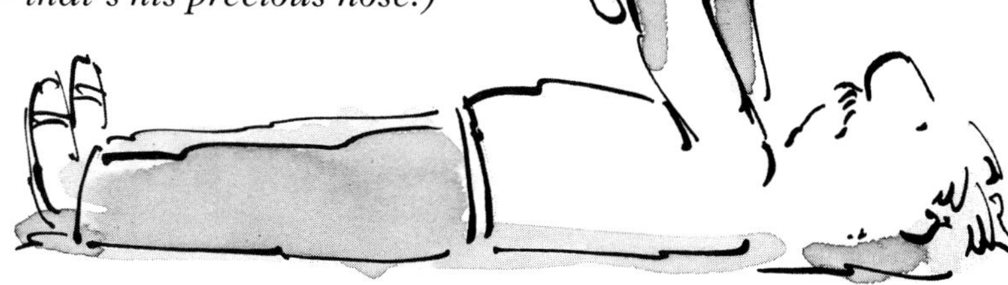

Thy father's pride and hope!
(He'll break the mirror with that skipping-rope!)
With pure heart newly stamped from Nature's mint
(Where did *he learn that squint?)*
Thou young domestic dove!
(He'll have that jug off, with another shove!)
Dear nursling of the hymeneal nest!
(Are those torn clothes his best?)
Little epitome of man!
(He'll climb upon the table, that's his plan!)
Touched with the beauteous tints of dawning life –
(He's got a knife!)

Thou enviable being!
No storms, no clouds, in thy blue sky foreseeing,
Play on, play on,
My elfin John!
Toss the light ball – bestride the stick –
(I knew so many cakes would make his sick!)
With fancies buoyant as the thistledown,
Prompting the face grotesque, and antic brisk,
With many a lamblike frisk –
(He's got the scissors, snipping at your gown!)

Thou pretty opening rose!
(Go to your mother, child, and wipe your nose!)
Balmy, and breathing music like the South,
(He really brings my heart into my mouth!)

Fresh as the morn, and brilliant as its star –
(I wish that window had an iron bar!)
Bold as the hawk, yet gentle as the dove –
(I tell you what, my love,
I cannot write, unless he's sent above!)

THOMAS HOOD *Blackwood's Magazine*, Feb. 1837

A Serenade

'Lullaby, oh, lullaby!'
Thus I heard a father cry,
'Lullaby, oh, lullaby!
The brat will never shut an eye;
Hither come, some power divine!
Close his lids or open mine!

'Lullaby, oh, lullaby!
What the devil makes him cry?
Lullaby, oh, lullaby!
Still he stares – I wonder why?
Why are not the sons of earth
Blind, like puppies from the birth?

'Lullaby, oh, lullaby!
Thus I heard the father cry;
'Lullaby, oh, lullaby!
Mary, you must come and try! –
Hush, oh hush, for mercy's sake –
The more I sing, the more you wake!

'Lullaby, oh, lullaby!
Fie, you little creature, fie;
Lullaby, oh, lullaby!
Is no poppy-syrup nigh?
Give him some, or give him all,
I am nodding to his fall!

'Lullaby, oh, lullaby!
Two such nights, and I shall die!
Lullaby, oh, lullaby!
He'll be bruised, and so shall I, –
How can I from bedposts keep,
When I'm walking in my sleep?'

'Lullaby, oh, lullaby!
Sleep his very looks deny –
Lullaby, oh, lullaby!
Nature soon will stupify –
My nerves relax, my eyes grow dim –
Who's that fallen – me or him?

THOMAS HOOD *Comic Annual*, 1837

Mrs Nickleby explains to Kate why the fine warm summer's day reminds her of roast pig:

'Roast pig; let me see. On the day five weeks after you were christened, we had a roast – no, that couldn't have been a pig, either, because there were a pair of them to carve, and your poor papa and I could never have thought of sitting down to two pigs – they must have been partridges. Roast pig! I hardly think we ever could have had one, now I come to remember, for your papa could never bear the sight of them in the shops, and used to say that they always put him in mind of very little babies, only the pigs had much fairer complexions; and he had a horror of little babies, too, because he couldn't very well afford any increase to his family, and had a natural dislike to the subject.'

DICKENS *Nicholas Nickleby*, 1839, ch. 41

Willie Winkie

Wee Willie Winkie rins through the town,
Up stairs and doon stairs in his nicht-gown,
Tirling at the window, crying at the lock,
Are the weans in their bed, for it's now ten o'clock.

Hey, Willie Winkie, are ye coming ben?
The cat's singing grey thrums to the sleeping hen,
The dog's spelder'd on the floor, and disna gi'e a cheep,
But here's a waukrife laddie! that winna fa' asleep.

Onything but sleep, you rogue! glow'ring like the moon,
Rattling in an airn jug wi' an airn spoon,
Rumbling, tumbling round about, crawing like a cock,
Skirling like a kenna-what, wauk'ning sleeping fock.

Hey, Willie Winkie – the wean's in a creel!
Wambling aff a bodie's knee like a very eel,
Rugging at the cat's lug, and raveling a' her thrums –
Hey, Willie Winkie – see, there he comes!

Wearied is the mither that has a stoorie wean,
A wee stumpie stoussie, that canna rin his lane,
That has a battle aye wi' sleep before he'll close an ee –
But a kiss frae aff his rosy lips gi'es strength anew to me.

WILLIAM MILLER *Whistle-Binkie*, 1841

Tirling, rattling *ben*, in *spelder'd*, stretched out
waukrife, wakeful *in a creel*, in a tizzy *stoorie*, restless
rin his lane, run alone

I had a rum go in a 'buss on Saturday. Streets being sloppy, and wantin' to go to my snuff-merchant in the Minories, I got into a 'buss at the foot of Holborn Hill, and seated myself next a pretty young woman with a child in her arms. Stopping at Bow Church, she asked if I'd have the kindness to hold the babby for a minute, when out she got, and cut down the court as hard as ever she could go. On went the 'buss, and I saw I was in for a plant. A respectable old gentleman, in black shorts and a puddingey white tie, sat opposite; and as the 'buss pulled up at the Mansion-house, I said, 'Perhaps you'd have the kindness to hold the babby for a minute, while I alight;' and popping it into his lap, I jumped out, making for Bucklersbury, threading all the courts in my line till I got back to Lincoln's Inn.

SURTEES *Handley Cross*, II, 1843, ch. 7

Invaluable Hints to Nurses and Nursemaids

If the darlings make a noise,
And a word or two don't stop 'em,
Pinch them if they're girls, if boys,
Make no more ado but 'whop' 'em.

Should the little dears resist,
When in suds too hot you dip 'em,
In their faces shake your fist,
If they dare to squall, then whip 'em.

When you comb their tangled hair,
Never mind their kicks and bawling,
You don't feel it, tug and tear,
If they're cheeky, send 'em sprawling.

And should Missus rush up stairs,
Frightened by the horrid rumpus,
Say, you never saw such bears,
Thus to treat their poor nurse Bumpus.

Then, when Madam's gone away,
If with vengeance you are foaming,
Just to show who's Missus, eh?
Give the cubs another combing.

If for three weeks by her cot,
Watching that cross peevish Minnie
Not a wink of sleep you've got,
Stand it longer – you're a ninny.

All my eye the doctor's stuff,
You've a dodge worth two on't, may be,
Poppy syrup's cheap enough,
'Bump' must sleep as well as baby.

And if Minnie's little hearse
Weeping neighbours soon set eyes on,
Who'll suppose, with such a nurse,
Minnie died of taking *pison*?

Punch, 17 February 1855

Perambulators and Pedestrians

Or, Mr Crosswig's Annoyance

What a lot of nasty little ugly babies in the streets,
Being wheeled about in those confounded little chairs one meets!
I mean those Perambulators, pushed by stupid, careless, blind,
Lazy, dawdling, idle, addle-headed servant girls behind.

Little screaming chits of creatures, little wryfaced roaring brats,
With their little absurd bows and feathers in their silly hats,
Foolish little coats and jackets, flimsy little fancy frocks,
Chubby faces, turned-up noses, and preposterous curly locks!

Slummaking untidy slatterns, moonstruck idiotic sluts,
Gazing, open-mouthed, upon the Grenadier who yonder
struts,
Staring at the linen-drapers' shops, or into vacant air,
Looking every way, except the way you're going with your
chair!

Howling loud your goblin charge is, all the while for rage or
fright,
If you've two they cuff each other, pinch, and kick, and
scratch and bite;
And, whilst you go blundering on, with zigzag course and
wandering wits,
Probably your blessed babes are struggling in convulsive
fits.

Not perceiving any object which is right before your nose,
Bolt ahead you drive your carriage on unhappy people's
toes,
Crushing corns and bunions, so that those who watch your
heedless path,
Will observe it marked by victims dancing mad with pain
and wrath.

I myself, Sir, I was looking at some prints the other day,
Standing quite, I do assure you, out of everybody's way;
Bang against my outer ankle a Perambulator drove:
Sir, it hurt me like Old Harry; grazed the skin off, Sir, by
Jove!

She – the trull – the wench who did it – there was she, a
goggle-eyed,
Gape-mouthed hoyden, staring one way this, and one the
other side,
Not a word to ask my pardon, not a word, Sir, uttered she,
On she went, and took no notice, as I limped and writhed,
of me.

Had she, while she was about it, pushed the babes between
my legs,
Bringing down my weight upon them as upon a nest of
eggs,
Warning would to foolish mothers by their fate have been
supplied,
And in those Perambulators wretched infants would not
ride.

Punch, 26 July 1856

Slummaking, slovenly

Abstractedly, I have no tendre for them till they have become a little human; an ugly baby is a very nasty object – and the prettiest is frightful when undressed – till about four months; in short as long as they have their big body and little limbs and that terrible frog-like action.

QUEEN VICTORIA Letter to the Princess Royal, 2 May 1859

The Baby in the House

The Doctor

'A finer than your newborn child,'
The Doctor said, 'I never saw,'
And I, but half believing, smiled
To think he thought me jolly raw.
And then I viewed the crimson thing,
And listened to its doleful squeal,
And rather wished the nurse would bring
The pap-boat with its earliest meal.
My wife remarked, 'I fear, a snub,'
The Doctor, 'Madam, never fear,'
''Tis hard, Ma'am, in so young a cub
To say.' Then Nurse, 'A cub? a Dear!'

The Glove

''Twere meet you tied the knocker up,'
The Doctor laughed, and said 'Goodbye,
And till you drown that yelping pup
Your lady will not close an eye.'
Then round I sauntered to the mews,
And Ponto heard his fate was near –
How few of coachmen will refuse
A crown to spend in beastly beer!
And then I bought a white kid glove,
Lucina's last and favourite sign,
Wound it the knocker's brass above,
And tied it with a piece of twine.

The Advertisement

'But, Love,' she said, in gentle voice,
('Twas ever delicate and low),
'The fact which makes our hearts rejoice
So many folks would like to know.
My Scottish cousins, on the Clyde,
Your uncle at Northavering Gap,
The Adams's at Morningside,
And Jane, who sent me up the cap.
So do.' The new commencing life
The *Times* announced, 'May 31,
At 16, Blackstone Place, the wife
of Samuel Bobchick, of a son.'

The Godfathers

'Of course your father must be one,'
Jemima said, in thoughtful tones;
'But what's the use of needy Gunn,
And I detest that miser Jones.'
I hinted Brown. 'Well, Brown would do,
But then his wife's a horrid Guy.'
De Blobbins? 'Herds with such a crew.'
Well, love, whom have you in your eye?
'Dear Mr Burbot.' Yes, he'll stand,
And as you say, he's seventy-three,
Rich, childless, hates that red-nosed band
Of nephews – Burbot let it be.

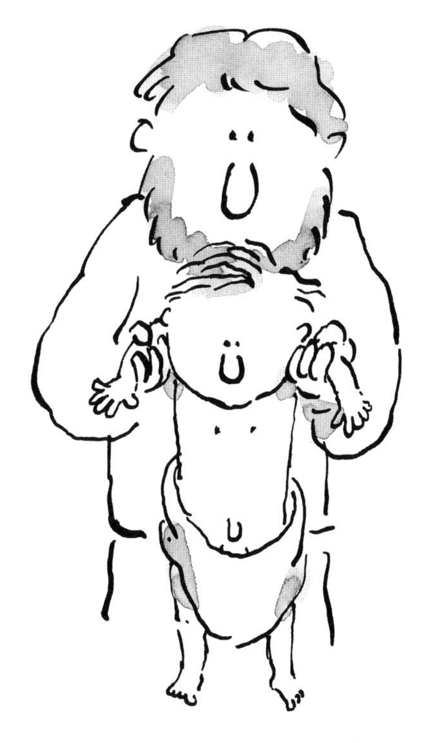

The Godmother

'We ought to ask your sister Kate,'
'Indeed, I shan't,' Jemima cried,
'She's given herself such airs of late,
I'm out of patience with her pride.
Proud that her squinting husband (Sam,
You know I hate that little sneak)
Has got a post at Amsterdam,
Where luckily he goes next week.
No, never ask of kin and kith,
We'll have that wife of George Bethune's,
Her husband is a silver-smith,
And she'll be sure to give some spoons.'

The Christening

'I sign him,' said the Curate, Howe,
O'er Samuel Burbot George Bethune,
Then baby kicked up such a row,
As terrified that Reverend coon.
The breakfast was a stunning spread,
As e'er confectioner sent in,
And playfully my darling said,
'Sam costs papa no end of tin.'
We laughed, made speeches, drank for joy:
Champagne hath stereoscopic charms;
For when Nurse brought our little boy,
I saw two Babies in her arms.

SHIRLEY BROOKS *Punch*, 8 September 1860: parody of Coventry Patmore's 'Angel in the House'

snub, snub nose

Punch and Judy's Baby

Punch (sits down and sings to the baby) –

Hush-a-by, baby, upon the tree-top,
When the wind blows the cradle will rock;
When the bough breaks the cradle will fall,
Down comes the baby and cradle and all.

Baby cries.

Punch (Shaking it.) What a cross boy! *(He lays it down on the play-board, and rolls it backwards and forwards, to rock it to sleep, and sings again.)*

Oh, slumber, my darling, thy sire is a knight,
Thy mother's a lady so lovely and bright;
The hills and the dales, and the tow'rs which you see,
They all shall belong, my dear creature, to thee.

(Punch continues rocking the child. It still cries, and he takes it up in his arms, saying, What a cross child! I can't a-bear cross children. *Then he vehemently shakes it, and knocks its head up against the side of the proceedings several times, representing to kill it, and he then throws it out of the winder.)*

Enter JUDY

Judy Where's the baby?

Punch (In a lemoncholy tone.) I have had a misfortune; the child was so terrible cross, I throwed it out of the winder. *(Lemontation of Judy for the loss of her dear child. She goes into asterisks, and then excites and fetches a cudgel, and commences beating Punch over the head.)*

From a punchman's description in *London Labour and the London Poor*, Henry Mayhew, vol. III, 1861

Aboriginal Poems for Infant Minds

Chackaboo, chickaboo, chuckaboo, chew,
Mark baby over with pretty tattoo;
Cut in the pattern like open-work tart:
Rub in the powder, and make baby smart.

Tattoo him, tattoo him, artist-man,
So we will, father, as fast as we can,
Prick him, and prick him, and mark him with V,
For the name of the Queen that lives over the sea.

What, cry when I'd cook you, not like to be stewed?
Then go and be raw, and not fit to be food.
Until you leave off, and I see that you've smiled,
I shan't take the trouble to eat such a child.

SHIRLEY BROOKS *Punch*, 30 March 1861

. . . she can sit at ease and pay her way;
A sober husband, too – a cheerful man –
Honest as ever stepped, and fond of her;
Yet she is never easy, never glad,
Because she has not children. Well-a-day!
If she could know how hard her mother worked,
And what ado I had, and what a moil
With my half-dozen! Children, ay, forsooth,
They bring their own love with them when they
  come,
But if they come not there is peace and rest;
The pretty lambs! and yet she cries for more:
Why, the world's full of them, and so is heaven –
They are not rare.

JEAN INGELOW 'Supper at the Mill' in *Poems*, 1863

If you rock an empty cradle, you will rock a new baby into it. This is a superstition *in viridi observantiâ*, and it is quite curious to see the face of alarm with which a poor woman, with her tenth baby in her arms, will dash across a room to prevent the 'baby-but-one' from engaging in such a dangerous amusement as rocking the empty cradle.

The Book of Days, Robert Chambers, 1864, II, 9 July

The Royal Baby

Oh, January Sixty-four,
Will be remembered evermore,
By old and young, by rich and poor,
For it brought a Royal Baby.
How nature every thing defies,
It took all England by surprise,
And people scarce believed their eyes,
On seeing the papers advertise
That Fortune turned the Royal scales
In favour of a Line of Males,
And actually the Prince of Wales –
Was Father of a Baby!

At Frogmore there was such a shine,
For there was not the remotest sign
That about two months before its time
Would come a Royal Baby;
In fact the Princess on that day
Felt only in the usual way,
And went upon the Ice quite gay
To see her husband Hockey play;
Now was it the excitement there
Was more than the Princess could bear,
Or was it something in the air
That disturbed the Royal Baby?

They shortly telegraphed to town
For the royal doctors to come down,
But there was not time, so Doctor Brown

Was called to attend the baby;
And when the child was brought to sight
They'd nothing to cover the little mite,
And the Princess said it served him right
For coming thus without invite;
If he would in such a hurry come
He must wait till something could be done
In the way of shirts, if 'twas only one
Of his father's, for the baby.

From Marlborough House came forth a Bale
Of infant togs to go by rail,
In a special train, they called it '*Mail*',
In honour of the baby;
The medical gents too, by that train,
All did their best to Frogmore gain,
But the baby made it all in vain,
For he would not wait until they came;
At length arrived, and when they knew
It was all over and they'd nought to do,
They all at *Brown* looked very *Blue*
And jealous about the baby.

The 'Daily Telegraph' with joy
Said 'nine pounds weighed the Royal boy'.
Now was that avoirdupois or troy –
The weight of the Royal baby?
Or is weight a necessary thing
For history in a future king,
For fear that some mean hireling
Might artfully the changes ring?

If the papers to this length will go
I expect to see in a day or so
That he's tried his strength and he's going to blow,
To try his lungs, this baby.

Earl Granville happened to be there,
Some shooting with the Prince to share,
And saw the doctor bag a *Heir* –
To the throne, a Royal baby;
The Countess Macclesfield, who,
With all good feeling, buckled to,
Had been in the mess, so of course she knew
Exactly what there was to do,
And the thanks of all the Court she'll share
For treating with such tender care
The first *pip* of a Windsor 'pair',
The Prince of Wales's baby.

But since it's all about the child
These simple lines have been compiled,
Now let me speak in accents mild
Of the parents of the baby;
May health and wealth them both befriend,
And happiness them each attend,
May Providence its blessings send,
And love their hearts for ever blend,
And may our Queen, their mother, reign
For years to see the Royal chain
Lengthened and strengthened in the main –
Each link a Royal baby.

Music-hall song. Words by C. H. WITT, Esq. Sung by 'The Great Vance' soon after the birth of Prince Albert Victor on 8 January 1864

Pig and Pepper

The door led right into a large kitchen, which was full of smoke from one end to the other: the Duchess was sitting on a three-legged stool in the middle, nursing a baby; the cook was leaning over the fire, stirring a large cauldron which seemed to be full of soup.

'There's certainly too much pepper in that soup!' Alice said to herself, as well as she could for sneezing.

There was certainly too much of it in the air. Even the Duchess sneezed occasionally; and the baby was sneezing and howling alternately without a moment's pause. The only things in the kitchen that did not sneeze, were the cook, and a large cat which was sitting on the hearth and grinning from ear to ear.

'Please would you tell me,' said Alice a little timidly, for she was not quite sure whether it was good manners for her to speak first, 'why your cat grins like that!'

'It's a Cheshire cat,' said the Duchess, 'and that's why. Pig!'

She said the last word with such sudden violence that Alice quite jumped; but she saw in another moment that it was addressed to the baby, and not to her, so she took courage, and went on again:-

'I didn't know that Cheshire cats always grinned; in fact, I didn't know that cats *could* grin.'

'They all can,' said the Duchess; 'and most of 'em do.'

'I don't know of any that do,' Alice said very politely, feeling quite pleased to have got into a conversation.

'You don't know much,' said the Duchess; 'and that's a fact.'

Alice did not at all like the tone of this remark, and thought it would be as well to introduce some other subject of conversation. While she was trying to fix on one, the cook took the cauldron of soup off the fire, and at once set to work throwing everything within her reach at the Duchess and the baby – the fire-irons came first; then followed a shower of saucepans, plates, and dishes. The Duchess took no notice of them even when they hit her; and the baby was howling so much already, that it was quite impossible to say whether the blows hurt it or not.

'Oh, *please* mind what you're doing!' cried Alice, jumping up and down in an agony of terror. 'Oh, there goes his *precious* nose;' as an unusually large saucepan flew close by it, and very nearly carried it off.

'If everybody minded their own business,' the Duchess said in a hoarse growl, 'the world would go round a deal faster than it does.'

'Which would *not* be an advantage,' said Alice, who felt very glad to get an opportunity of showing off a little of her knowledge. 'Just think what work it would make with the day and night! You see the earth takes twenty-four hours to turn round on its axis—'

'Talking of axes,' said the Duchess, 'chop off her head.'

Alice glanced rather anxiously at the cook, to see if she meant to take the hint; but the cook was busily engaged in stirring the soup, and did not seem to be listening, so she ventured to go on again: 'Twenty-four hours, I *think*; or is it twelve? I—'

'Oh, don't bother *me*,' said the Duchess; 'I never could abide figures!' And with that she began nursing her child again, singing a sort of lullaby to it as she did so, and giving it a violent shake at the end of every line:

'Speak roughly to your little boy
And beat him when he sneezes;
He only does it to annoy,
Because he knows it teases.'

CHORUS
(In which the cook and the baby joined):–
'Wow! wow! wow!'

While the Duchess sang the second verse of the song, she kept tossing the baby violently up and down, and the poor little thing howled so, that Alice could hardly hear the words:–

'I speak severely to my boy,
I beat him when he sneezes;
For he can thoroughly enjoy
The pepper when he pleases!'

CHORUS
'Wow! wow! wow!'

'Here! you may nurse it a bit, if you like!' the Duchess said to Alice, flinging the baby at her as she spoke. 'I must go and get ready to play croquet with the Queen,' and she hurried out of the room. The cook threw a frying-pan after her as she went out, but it just missed her.

Alice caught the baby with some difficulty, as it was a queer-shaped little creature, and held out its arms and legs in all directions, 'just like a star-fish,' thought Alice. The poor little thing was snorting like a steam-engine when she caught it, and kept doubling itself up and straightening itself out again, so that altogether, for the first minute or two, it was as much as she could do to hold it.

As soon as she had made out the proper way of nursing it, (which was to twist it up into a sort of knot, and then keep tight hold of its right ear and left foot, so as to prevent its undoing itself,) she carried it out into the open air. 'If I don't take this child away with me,' thought Alice, 'they're sure to kill it in a day or two: wouldn't it be murder to leave it behind?' She said the last words out loud, and the little thing grunted in reply (it had left off sneezing by this time). 'Don't grunt,' said Alice; 'that's not at all a proper way of expressing yourself.'

The baby grunted again, and Alice looked very anxiously into its face to see what was the matter with it. There could be no doubt that it had a *very* turn-up nose, much more like a snout than a real nose; also its eyes were getting extremely small for a baby: altogether Alice did not like the look of the thing at all . . .

Alice was just beginning to think to herself, 'Now, what am I to do with this creature when I get it home?' when it grunted again, so violently, that she looked down into its face in some alarm. This time there could be *no* mistake about it: it was neither more nor less than a pig.

LEWIS CARROLL *Alice's Adventures in Wonderland*, 1865

Nurse being compelled to leave me, I was left sole manager of an infant, with no notion of 'how to do it'. Nurse had always improvised a bed for him beside hers. It was but two pillows placed in two armchairs, with their seats facing. She had insisted upon having new warm blankets, and no sheets, for him to sleep in – indeed, his pillow was covered with soft flannel. I saw all this, certainly with a species of contempt for what I was tempted to think almost *uncanny* ways, which I altered as soon as she left.

The first night after her departure my boy lay in my arms until we went to bed. It was a novelty to have him entirely to ourselves. I could not hug him enough; and in the exuberance of my unlimited affection had almost forgotten his supper, cooked by our maid-servant in the kitchen, which, when it came, had a suspicious blackness, and it was undeniably smoky. However, babe can't taste that, I thought; but didn't he, though? The yell he set up was piercing, very suggestive of pins and needles all over him. Arthur fidgeted about while I stuffed the child with as much food as I thought necessary, which the little obstinate thing rejected a

moment after, and would have a perverse attack of hiccups; so that I had to place him across my shoulder and beat his back, to the utter detriment of my silk dress. By dint of much perseverance he was quieted and slept. Now, thought I, he shall lie in the refreshing cool sheets. Five minutes only of this treatment sufficed to drown our ears with his persistent cries.

'What is the matter?' Arthur pettishly exclaimed. 'Unfasten him, Mary; he must have a pin sticking in him.'

I sat up in bed, and Arthur held the light while I examined him. No, there was nothing to cause his cries . . . I got him to sleep, and kept him on my arm close to me. After some time this constrained position prevented my sleeping, but the moment I attempted to dislodge him from his roost a fractious peevish cry was set up. This continued at intervals till nearly morning . . . Worn out with fatigue and sleeplessness . . . I was unable to get up, and my husband ate his breakfast in discontent – alone; and as if the spirit of mischief possessed the child, he now lay immoveable as a little log, quite regardless that I had turned him on to his father's pillow, and severed him from my protecting arms. The memory of that first night haunts me now.

MRS ELIZA WARREN *How I Managed My Children*, 1865, ch. 1

Mrs K., after expressing her love for her young children, added, tenderly, 'And how do *you* like babies, Mr Lamb?' His answer, immediate, almost precipitate, was 'Boi-boi-boiled, ma'am.'

Charles Lamb: a memoir, Barry Cornwall, 1866, ch. 7

To the Young Naturalist

It's a thing very proper and right in a child
To study the habits of animals wild.
Would you know how the beasts when at liberty sup?
And would satisfied be
If you only could see
How lions and tigers do *eat people up?*
As to give them yourself to eat, not such a gaby
Of course you would be. But there's always the baby!

THOMAS HOOD *Griset's Grotesques*, 1867

Hushaby, baby, sleep sound as a top,
While Jane goes and stares at that milliner's shop:
No doubt if you wake you will make a great squall,
But little she careth how loudly you bawl.

Punch, 7 November 1868

Hush-a-bye, baby, your milk's in the tin,
Mummy has got you a nice sitter-in;
Hush-a-bye, baby now don't get a twinge
While Mummy and Daddy are out on the binge.

ANON *Verse and Worse*, Arnold Silcock, 1952

The Precocious Baby
A Very True Tale

(To be sung to the Air of the 'Whistling Oyster')

An elderly person – a prophet by trade –
With his quips and tips
On withered old lips,
He married a young and beautiful maid;
The cunning old blade!
Though rather decayed,
He married a beautiful, beautiful maid.

She was only eighteen, and as fair as could be,
With her tempting smiles
And maidenly wiles,
And he was a trifle off seventy-three:
Now what could she see
Is a puzzle to me,
In a buffer of seventy – seventy-three!

Of all their acquaintances bidden (or bad)
With their loud high jinks
And underbred winks,
None thought they'd a family have – but they had;
A dear little lad
Who drove 'em half mad,
For he turned out a horribly fast little cad.

For when he was born he astonished all by,
With their 'Law, dear me!'
'Did ever you see?'
He'd a weed in his mouth and a glass in his eye,
A hat all awry –
An octagon tie –
And a miniature – miniature glass in his eye.

He grumbled at wearing a frock and a cap,
With his 'Oh, dear, oh!'
And his 'Hang it! you know!'
And he turned up his nose at his excellent pap –
'My friend, it's a tap
That is not worth a rap.'
(Now this was remarkably excellent pap.)

He'd chuck his nurse under the chin, and he'd say,
With his 'Fal, lal, lal' –
You doosed fine gal!'
This shocking precocity drove 'em away:
'A month from today
Is as long as I'll stay –
Then I'd wish, if you please, for to hook it away.'

His father, a simple old gentleman, he
With nursery rhyme
And 'Once on a time,'
Would tell him the story of 'Little Bo-P,'
'So pretty was she,
So pretty and wee,
As pretty, as pretty, as pretty could be.'

But the babe, with a dig that would startle an ox,
With his 'C'ck! Oh, my! –
Go along wiz 'oo, fie!'
Would exclaim, 'I'm affaid 'oo a socking ole fox.'
Now a father it shocks,
And it whitens his locks,
When his little babe calls him a shocking old fox.

The name of his father he'd couple and pair
(With his ill-bred laugh,
And insolent chaff)
With those of the nursery heroines rare –
Virginia the Fair,
Or Good Goldenhair,
Till the nuisance was more than a prophet could bear.

'There's Jill and White Cat' (said the bold little brat,
With his loud, 'Ha, ha!')
''Oo sly ickle Pa!
Wiz 'oo Beauty, Bo-peep, and 'oo Mrs Jack Sprat!
I've noticed 'oo pat
My *pretty White Cat –*
I sink dear mamma ought to know about dat!'

He early determined to marry and wive,
For better or worse
With his elderly nurse –
Which the poor little boy didn't live to contrive:
His health didn't thrive –
No longer alive,
He died an enfeebled old dotard at five!

MORAL

Now elderly men of the bachelor crew,
With wrinkled hose
And spectacled nose,
Don't marry at all – you may take it as true
If ever you do
The step you will rue,
For your babes will be elderly – elderly too.

W. S. GILBERT *The Bab Ballads*, 1869

Elder of Fourteen 'Where's baby, Madge?'
Madge 'In the other room, I think, Emily.'
Elder of Fourteen 'Go directly, and see what she's doing, and tell her she mustn't!'

Punch, 16 November 1872

Under This sOd our Babie Lies
It neither cRies nOr HolErs
IT LivEd Just twenty 7 Days
And cost us $40

Epitaph from a tombstone in Indiana

Nurses and motherly elder sisters are apt to make everything give way to the baby-pet, and allow it to become the torment of the older children, whose toys are taken away to gratify its destructiveness, and whose important little occupations are violently broken up to gratify its volatile spirit of imitation and curiosity. To the elders, the threading of beads, or daubing of pictures, or making of models, may seem even less important than baby's gratification; but to the child they are the business of life, pursued with a sense of purpose and industry, and it is both harsh and mischievous to sacrifice them uniformly to the little one. True, he is very likely to squall, and obstinately insist on being amused with nothing but invading the occupation that engrosses the older one; and the child may be advised – but so as to leave it entirely a matter of free-will – to give way to him or else put the coveted object out of sight . . . If possible children of this more reasonable age ought to have some refuge from the meddlesomeness of the lesser ones.

C. M. YONGE *Womankind*, 1876, ch. 4

Mrs Winslow's Soothing Syrup

I am a happy married man,
And I could dance with joy,
For my dear wife's presented me
With such a bouncing boy;
At first he cried the whole night long,
And no one in the house
Could get a wink of sleep; but now
He's quiet as a mouse.

(*Spoken*) And all through Mrs Winslow's soothing syrup! Bless her for inventing it! she deserves a putty medal, because it's all through her that –

Chorus:
I've found a way to soothe the blessed baby,
No more at night a father need get wild.
Now I can sing or dance a hornpipe maybe,
Right overhead or on the bed, I never wake the child.

When baby's had his little bath
And mammy's wiped him dry,
And powdered him with what I've seen
My wife use on the sly,
She gives him just a little dose,
Which sends him off to sleep,
And, thanks to Misses Winslow's art,
All night he'll quiet keep.

(*Spoken*) Half a spoonful in a wine glass full of water, and the seven sleepers ain't in the hunt. Hooray for Mrs Winslow, for –

Chorus:
I've found a way, etc.

Last week, it's only happened once,
I came in rather late,
And climbing up two flights of stairs
I seemed to fall down eight;
That never woke the baby though
My wife made a to-do,
And made me wish she'd had a dose
Of Mrs Winslow's too.

(*Spoken*) Only a small dose, you know, on club nights. Keep the big doses for mothers-in-law, half a tumbler three times a-day; that'll make 'em fall off into a gentle slumber directly they've made their wills.

Chorus:
I've found a way, etc.

I used to dread a family,
But now it will me please
To welcome them with open arms
In twos or even threes;
I do not care if we go on
As well as we've begun,
Hooray! for soothing syrup then,
I'll order half a ton.

Chorus:
I've found a way, etc.

Music-hall song. Words by W. R. GORDON, 1877

The Kid

My spirit, in the doorway's pause,
Fluttered with fancies in my breast;
Obsequious to all decent laws,
I felt exceedingly distressed.
I knew it rude to enter there
With Mrs V. in such a state;
And, 'neath a magisterial air,
Felt actually indelicate.
I knew the nurse began to grin;
I turned to greet my Love. Said she –
'Confound your modesty, come in!
– What shall we call the darling, V.?'
(There are so many charming names!
Girls' – Peg, Moll, Doll, Fan, Kate,
Blanche, Bab:
Boys' – Mahershalal-hashbaz, James,
Luke, Nick, Dick, Mark, Aminadab.)

Lo, as the acorn to the oak,
As well-heads to the river's height,
As to the chicken the moist yolk,
As to high noon the day's first white –
Such is the baby to the man.
There, straddling one red arm and leg,
Lay my last work, in length a span,
Half hatched, and conscious of the egg.
A creditable child, I hoped;
And half a score of joys to be
Through sunny lengths of prospect sloped
Smooth to the bland futurity.
O, fate surpassing other dooms,
O, hope above all wrecks of time!
O, light that fills all vanquished glooms,
O, silent song o'ermastering rhyme!

I covered either little foot,
I drew the strings about its waist;
Pink as the unshell'd inner fruit,
But barely decent, hardly chaste,
Its nudity had startled me;
But when the petticoats were on,
'I know,' I said; 'It's name shall be
Paul Cyril Athanasius John.'
'Why,' said my wife, 'the child's a girl.'
My brain swooned, sick with failing sense;
With all perception in a whirl,
How could I tell the difference?
'Nay,' smiled the nurse, 'the child's a boy.'
And all my soul was soothed to hear

That so it was: then startled Joy
Mocked Sorrow with a doubtful tear.

And I was glad as one who sees
For sensual optics things unmeet:
As purity makes passion freeze,
So faith warns science off her beat.
Blessed are they that have not seen,
And yet, not seeing, have believed:
To walk by faith, as preached the Dean,
And not by sight, have I achieved.
Let love, that does not look, believe;
Let knowledge, that believes not, look:
Truth pins her trust on falsehood's sleeve,
While reason blunders by the book.

Then Mrs Prig addressed me thus:
'Sir, if you'll be advised by me,
You'll leave the blessed babe to us;
It's my belief he wants his tea.'

SWINBURNE *The Heptalogia*, 1880

My Baby

I'm the father of an infant,
   Baby mine, baby mine;
He won't let me rest an instant,
   Baby mine, baby mine;
He won't do a thing he's bid,
How I wish that I was rid
Of that awful sassy kid,
   Baby mine, baby mine,
Of that awful sassy kid,
   Baby mine.

At my meals I have to hold him,
   Baby mine, baby mine;
But I never dare to scold him,
   Baby mine, baby mine;
My face he'll surely scratch,
And the table-cloth he'll snatch,
All my crockery goes smash,
   Baby mine, baby mine,
All my crockery goes smash,
   Baby mine.

In my hair he often lingers,
   Baby mine, baby mine;
With molasses on his fingers,
   Baby mine, baby mine;
You ought to hear him roar,
While I have to walk the floor,
Oh, I'd like to break his jaw,

Baby mine, baby mine,
Yes, I'd like to break his jaw,
Baby mine.

Sung by CHARLIE BACKUS at the San Francisco
Minstrels' Opera House, *c.* 1880

An Algonquin Legend

How the Lord of Men and Beasts strove with the Mighty Wasis, and was shamefully defeated

Now it came to pass when Glooskap had conquered all his enemies, even the *Kewahqu'*, who were giants and sorcerers, and the *m'téoulin*, who were magicians, and the *Pamola*, who is the evil spirit of the night air, and all manner of ghosts, witches, devils, cannibals, and goblins, that he thought upon what he had done, and wondered if his work was at an end.

And he said this to a certain woman. But she replied, 'Not so fast, Master, for there yet remains One whom no one has ever conquered or got the better of in any way, and who will remain unconquered to the end of time.'

'And who is he?' inquired the Master.

'It is the mighty *Wasis*,' she replied, 'and there he sits; and I warn you that if you meddle with him you will be in sore trouble.'

Now *Wasis* was the Baby. And he sat on the floor sucking a piece of maple-sugar, greatly contented, troubling no one.

As the Lord of Men and Beasts had never married or had a child, he knew naught of the way of managing children. Therefore he was quite certain, as is the wont of such people, that he knew all about it. So he turned to Baby with a bewitching smile and bade him come to him.

Then Baby smiled again, but did not budge. And the Master spake sweetly and made his voice like that of the summer bird, but it was of no avail, for Wasis sat still and sucked his maple-sugar.

Then the Master frowned and spoke terribly, and ordered Wasis to come crawling to him immediately. And Baby burst out into crying and yelling, but did not move for all that.

Then, since he could do but one thing more, the Master had recourse to magic. He used his most awful spells, and sang the songs which raise the dead and scare the devils. And Wasis sat and looked on admiringly, and seemed to find it very interesting, but all the same he never moved an inch.

So Glooskap gave it up in despair, and Wasis, sitting on the floor in the sunshine, went *goo! goo!* and crowed.

And to this day when you see a babe well contented, going *goo! goo!* and crowing, and no one can tell why, know that it is because he remembers the time when he overcame the Master who had conquered all the world. For of all the beings that have ever been since the beginning, Baby is alone the only invincible one.

Algonquin Legends of New England,
Charles G. Leland, 1884

The bell is rung, and somebody sent to tell nurse to bring down. This is the signal for all the females present to commence talking 'baby', during which time you are left to your own sad thoughts, and to speculations upon the practicability of suddenly recollecting an important engagement, and the likelihood of your being believed if you do. Just when you have concocted an absurdly implausible tale about a man outside, the door opens, and a tall, severe-looking woman enters, carrying what at first sight appears to be a particularly skinny bolster, with the feathers all at one end. Instinct, however, tells you that this is the baby, and you rise with a miserable attempt at appearing eager. When the first gush of feminine enthusiasm with which the object in question is received has died out, and the number of ladies talking at once has been reduced to the ordinary four or five, the circle of fluttering petticoats divides, and room is made for you to step forward. This you do with much the same air that you would walk into the dock at Bow Street, and then, feeling utterly miserable, you stand solemnly staring at the child. There is dead silence, and you know that every one is waiting for you to speak. You try to think of something to say, but find, to your horror, that your reasoning faculties have left you. It is a moment of despair, and your evil genius, seizing the opportunity, suggests to you some of the most idiotic remarks that it is possible for a human being to perpetrate. Glancing round with an imbecile smile, you sniggeringly observe that 'It hasn't got much hair, has it?' Nobody answers you for a minute, but at last the stately nurse says with much gravity – 'It is not customary for children five weeks old to have long hair.'

JEROME K. JEROME *Idle Thoughts of an Idle Fellow*, 1886

The Baby on the Shore

The sun was shining brightly,
Yes, shining as it never shone before;
We were thinking of the old folks at home
And we left the baby on the shore.
Yes, we left the baby on the shore,
A thing we've never done before;
Oh, way down upon the old Swanee river,
You will find the baby on the shore.

We are leaving, leaving now for ever,
A thing which we've never done before;
If you see the mother tell her gently,
She will find her baby on the shore . . .
If you see the mother tell her gently,
That we sat upon her baby on the shore.
The baby's quietly sleeping –
A thing which it never did before;
So, after all it is better
To leave the baby on the shore.

Part of GEORGE GROSSMITH's famous musical sketch
'How I Discovered America', 1894. 'To be played with
grace and sung with mock gravity.'

Lady Bracknell . . . Prism! Where is that baby?

Miss Prism Lady Bracknell, I admit with shame that I do not know. I only wish I did. The plain facts of the case are these. On the morning of the day you mention, a day that is for ever branded on my memory, I prepared as usual to take the baby out in its perambulator. I had also with me a somewhat old, but capacious hand-bag, in which I had intended to place the manuscript of a work of fiction that I had written during my few unoccupied hours. In a moment of mental abstraction, for which I never can forgive myself, I deposited the manuscript in the bassinette, and placed the baby in the hand-bag.

Jack (*Who has been listening attentively.*) But where did you deposit the hand-bag?

Miss Prism Do not ask me, Mr Worthing.

Jack Miss Prism, this is a matter of no small importance to me. I insist on knowing where you deposited the hand-bag that contained that infant.

Miss Prism I left it in the cloak-room of one of the larger railway stations in London.

Jack What railway station?

Miss Prism (*Quite crushed.*) Victoria. The Brighton line. (*Sinks into a chair.*)

OSCAR WILDE *The Importance of Being Earnest*, 1895, Act III.

Oh! let me kiss the baby
Once more before I go;
Oh! let me kiss the baby
And bite his little toe.

Traditional

'It occurred to Augustus Hare's[1] widow as just possible that my parents might be induced to give me up to her altogether, to live with her as her own child. In July she wrote her petition, and was almost surprised at the glad acceptance it met with. Mrs Hare's answer was very brief – 'My dear Maria, how very kind of you! Yes, certainly, the baby shall be sent as soon as it is weaned; and if any one else would like one, would you kindly recollect that we have others.'

AUGUSTUS HARE *The Story of my Life*, I, 1896

[1]The author's uncle.

There was no doubt that Mary was a very wonderful baby, because Pater took a great interest in her, and Pater was a very clever man and not likely to be taken in by a second rater. More than that, Pater had never been known to be partial to babies as a class, but he used to spend many hours of a cold winter's night, walking up and down in his red and yellow dressing-gown, with little Mary in his arms, singing her to sleep with 'Onward, Christian Soldiers', while she howled at the top of her voice. You may be sure Pater would not have done that for any ordinary baby.

HIS HONOUR JUDGE PARRY *The First Book of Krab*, 1897, 'The Clockwork Child'

When Roberta was first shown to her papa by the nurse, he was in despair, and ran and shut himself up in his studio, and, I believe, almost wept. He feared he had brought a monster into the world. He had always thought that female babies were born with large blue eyes framed with long lashes, a beautiful complexion of the lily and the rose, and their shining, flaxen curls already parted in the middle. And this little bald, wrinkled, dark-red, howling lump of humanity all but made him ill. But soon the doctor came and knocked at the door, and said –

'I congratulate you, old fellow, on having produced the most magnificent little she I ever saw in my life – bar none: she might be shown for money.'

And it turned out that this was not the coarse, unfeeling chaff poor Barty took it for at first, but the pure and simple truth.

GEORGE DU MAURIER *The Martian*, 1897, ch. 8

'In Rombolia every one grows the other way, and has done so for many years. They begin as old people, and grow down. How it answers I cannot say . . .'

'But if they go on growing that way,' said Kate, 'they will become long-clothes babies again.'

'No,' replied Miss Echo, 'not all of them. The sensible ones stop at about ten or twelve, but of course some think the younger they grow the happier they will be, and go on growing and growing until they do become long-clothes babies again, and then they get shipped off of course. They cannot do with a lot of squalling babies in Rombolia. Certainly not.'

'Poor little things,' said Kate tenderly.

'Oh, they are all right though,' said Miss Echo. 'There's a large demand for children of that sort somewhere, I suppose, and I expect they go where they are wanted, and so every one is pleased.'

HIS HONOUR JUDGE PARRY *The Scarlet Herring*, 1899,
'The Golden Jujube', ch. 4

Who took me from my nice warm cot,
And sat me on the cold cold pot
Whether I wanted to or not?
My Mother.

Parody of Ann Taylor's 'My Mother'

Presently a saddle of mutton was brought on the table. When Limby saw this he set up a crow of delight. 'Limby ride,' said he . . . 'Limby on – Limby ride on bone' . . .

'What an extraordinary child!' said the mother; 'how clever to know it was like a saddle – the little dear. No, no, Limby – grease frock Limby.'

But Limby cared nothing about a greasy frock, not he – he was used enough to that; and therefore roared out more lustily for a ride on the mutton . . . Limby made such a roaring, that neither father nor mother could get their dinners, and scarcely knew whether they were eating beef or mutton.

'It is impossible to let him ride on the mutton,' said his father: 'Quite impossible!'

'Well, but you might just put him astride the dish, just to satisfy him; you can take care his legs or clothes do not go into the gravy . . . it won't hurt the mutton.'

The father rose, and took Limby from his chair, and, with the greatest caution, held his son's legs astride, so that they might hang on each side of the dish without touching it; 'just to satisfy him,' as he said, 'that they might dine in quiet,' and was about to withdraw him from it immediately. But Limby was not to be cheated in that way, he wished to feel the saddle *under* him, and accordingly forced himself down upon it; but feeling it rather warmer than was agreeable, started, and lost his balance, and fell down among the dishes, soused in melted butter, cauliflower, and gravy – floundering, and kicking, and screaming, to the detriment of glasses, jugs, dishes, and everything else on the table.

'My child! my child!' said his mamma; 'O save my child!'

She snatched him up, and pressed his begreased garments

close to the bosom of her best silk gown. Neither father nor mother wanted any more dinner after this. As to Limby, he was as frisky afterwards as if nothing had happened; and, about half an hour from the time of this disaster, *cried for his dinner.*

The Bad Family, ed. E. V. Lucas, 1900,
'Limby Lumpy'

Would you believe it? – that boxish thing in the cellar, that H.O. wanted them to make a rabbit-hutch of – well, Mr Red House has cleaned it and mended it, and Mrs Red House took us up to the room where it was, to let us look at it again. And, unbelievable to relate, it turned out to have rockers, and some one in dark bygone ages seems, for reasons unknown to the present writer, to have wasted no end of carpentry and carving on it, just to make it into a *Cradle*. And what is more, since we were there last, Mr and Mrs Red House had succeeded in obtaining a small but quite alive baby to put in it.

I suppose they thought it was wilful waste to have a cradle and no baby to use it. But it could so easily have been used for something else. It would have made a ripping rabbit-hutch, and babies are far more trouble than rabbits to keep, and not nearly so profitable, I believe.

E. NESBIT *The New Treasure Seekers*, 1904,
'The Intrepid Explorer and his Lieutenant'

The examiner wished to get the children to express moral reprobation of lazy people, and he led up to it by asking who were the persons who got all they could and did nothing in return.

For some time there was silence, but at last one little girl, who had obviously reasoned out the answer from her own experiences, exclaimed with a good deal of confidence: 'Please, sir, it's the baby'.

Children's Answers, J. H. Burn, 1905

Holly-o, mistletoe,
Put the baby on the po!
When he's done, wipe his bum,
Tell his mummy what he's done.

Counting-out rhyme

Fudge, fudge, tell the judge,
Mother's had a baby.
It isn't a girl, it isn't a boy,
It's just an ordinary baby.
Wrap it up in tissue paper,
Put it in the elevator:
  First floor, stop,
  Second floor, stop,
  Third floor, stop.
  Fourth floor, kick him out the door –
  Mother hasn't got a baby any more!

American jump-rope rhyme

Over the garden wall,
I let the baby fall.
Mother came out and gave me a clout;
I asked her who she was bossing about,
She gave me another to match the other –
Over the garden wall.

Ball-bouncing rhyme

Miss Susie had a baby,
She named him Tiny Tim.
She put him in the bath tub
To see if he could swim.
He drank up all the water,
He ate up all the soap,
He tried to eat the bath tub
But it wouldn't go down his throat.

Miss Susie called the doctor,
The doctor called the nurse,
The nurse called the lady with the
alligator purse.

In came the doctor,
In came the nurse,
In came the lady with the
alligator purse.

'Measles' said the doctor,
'Mumps' said the nurse,
'Nothing' said the lady with the
alligator purse.

Wrong was the doctor,
Wrong was the nurse,
Right was the lady with the
alligator purse.

Out went the doctor,
Out went the nurse,
Out went the lady with the
alligator purse.

Clapping rhyme

Calculating Clara

O'er the rugged mountain's brow
Clara threw the twins she nursed,
And remarked, 'I wonder now
Which will reach the bottom first?'

HARRY GRAHAM *Ruthless Rhymes*, 1909

The Grizzly Bear is huge and wild;
He has devoured the infant child.
The infant child is not aware
It has been eaten by the bear.

A. E. HOUSMAN

Good-by Bill

Dollar Bill, that I've held so tight
Ever since payday, a week ago,
Shall I purchase with you tonight
A pair of seats at the vaudeville show?
(Hark! A voice from the easy chair:
'Look at his shoes! We must buy a pair.')

Dollar Bill, from the wreckage saved,
Tell me, how shall I squander you?
Shall I be shined, shampooed and shaved,
Singed and trimmed 'round the edges, too?
(Hark! A voice from the easy chair:
'He hasn't a romper that's fit to wear.')

Dollar Bill, that I cherished so,
Think of the cigarettes you'd buy,
Turkish ones, with a kick, you know:
Makin's eventually tire a guy.
(Hark! A voice from the easy chair:
'Look at those stockings! Just one big tear!)

Dollar Bill, it is time to part.
What do I care for a vaudeville show?
I'll shave myself and look just as smart.
Makins aren't so bad, you know.
Dollar Bill, we must say good-by:
There on the floor is the Reason Why.

RING W. LARDNER *Bib Ballads*, 1915

Johnnie in the Cradle

It was a man in a farm – a man and his wife – they were nae long married, ye see; and they'd a wee kiddie, and they christened its name Johnnie, see? But it was a very crabbit wee baby this, it was always goin' 'Nyaa, nyaa' a' the time, and never growin'.

There was another neighbourin' man, the tailor, used to come and visit this farmer. They used to always have a wee drink of whisky between them, ye see, and a game o' cards. And the wife wanted to go wi' the farmer to the market, so the tailor says 'I'll watch the wean, if she wants to go.'

So the tailor was there at the side of the fire, sewin' at a pair of trousers, and he hears a voice sayin', 'Is ma mother and faither awa?' The tailor didnae think but for one minute it was the baby that was talkin'. So he looks roond, he looks oot the windae, but he could see nothing. He goes back and sits in the chair again.

So he hears the voice sayin' again, 'Is ma mother an' ma faither awa tae the market? Are they away?' So he looks roond, and this was the baby haudin' its wee hands at each side o' the cradle; it was sittin' up. Of coorse, the tailor was kin' o' feared, but he says, 'Yes,' he says, 'they're away tae the market, Johnnie,' he says, 'What is it?' 'If you look in the press,' the baby says, 'there's a bottle o' whisky. Gie me a wee taste.' So the tailor took a taste o' the whisky, and teemed oot some for the wee baby.

So it says, 'Hae ye got a set o' pipes in the hoose?' 'Not me,' says the tailor, he says. 'Well,' it says, 'go oot to the byre and bring me in a strae, an I'll play you a tune.' So the tailor takes a straw in, and hands it tae Johnnie. He was worried, the tailor, noo; he was thinkin' about this wee Johnnie bein' the fairy, see? 'Can ye play a strae?' says the tailor. So the fairy says 'Aye', and it played the loveliest tune on the pipes that ever ye heard – through a strae!

So it says, 'Is it time for ma father and mother to come home yet? Ye better take a look an' see if they're comin'.' So the tailor looked oot the windae, and he says 'Aye, here they're comin' up the lane.' So the wee fairy, he says, 'I'll have tae get back into ma cradle again.' And when the mother come to the door the wee bairn started going again, 'Nyaa, nyaa', greetin' away, ye see?

So the tailor broke the news to the farmer, and he says to the farmer, 'You and your wife,' he says, 'let on there's another market, and that the stuff wasnae half sellit. But go into the byre, and lift the curtain back, and listen tae everything that's goin' on. Ye can see what I'm tellin' ye's true, it's a fairy ye've got for a wean.'

So, anyway, the next mornin' come, and they packed up their things, lettin' on they were goin' tae market. And they went through tae the byre, and they heard the wee fairy sayin' tae the tailor, 'Is ma mother and father away tae the market?' 'Oh yes,' he says, 'they're away to the market,' he says. 'Johnnie,' he says, 'you'll be wantin' a drink.' 'Aye, get the whisky oot,' he says, 'and gie me a drink.' Well, the woman nearly fainted when she heard her ain baby speakin' to the tailor, ye see?

The baby's father come in, and got the griddle. And the fairy looked wi' its eyes wild, and watched the father pittin' the griddle on the fire, seein' nae floor [flour] on the table – nae bread gettin' baked, ye see?

Next thing come in, was a half o' a bag o' horse manure. An' the farmer put some o' the horse manure on tap o' the griddle. And just as he was comin' forward to reach for wee Johnnie in the cradle, he made a jump up the lum, and he cries doon the chimley, 'I wish I had 'a kent my mother – if I'd 'a been longer wi' my mother,' he says, 'I would ha' liked to ken her better.'

Scottish folk tale

lum, chimney

Fifth Philosopher's Song

A million million spermatozoa,
All of them alive:
Out of their cataclysm but one poor Noah
Dare hope to survive.

And among that billion minus one
Might have chanced to be
Shakespeare, another Newton, a new Donne –
But the One was me.

Shame to have ousted your betters thus,
Taking ark while the others remained outside!
Better for all of us, froward Homunculus,
If you'd quietly died!

ALDOUS HUXLEY *Leda*, 1920

The Pixies' Baby

Once the pixies stole a baby,
But it's only fair to say
That they very soon returned it,
And on the very self-same day:
Who blames 'em?

ANON *Recitations*, ed. B. Heitland, 1919

While William was picking it up, it threw the pillow on to his head. Then it chuckled. William began to conceive an active dislike of it . . . He held the baby to his chest with both arms clasped tightly round its waist. Its feet dangled in the air. It occupied the time by kicking William in the stomach, pulling his hair, and putting its fingers in his eyes. 'It beats me,' panted William to himself, 'what people see in babies! Scratchin' an' kickin' and blindin' folks and pullin' their hair out!'

When he entered the barn he was greeted by a sudden silence.

'It's a kidnap,' said William, triumphantly. 'We'll get a ransom on it.'

They gazed at him in awed admiration. This was surely the cream of out-lawry. He set the infant on the ground where it toddled for a few steps and sat down suddenly and violently. It then stared fixedly at the tallest boy present and smiled seraphically.

'Dad-dad-dad-dad-dad!'

Douglas, the tallest boy, grinned sheepishly . . . With vague memories of his mother's treatment of infants, he . . . inserted a finger in its mouth. The infant happened to possess four front teeth, two upper and two lower, and they closed like a vice upon Douglas' finger. He was now examining the marks.

'Look! Right deep down! See it? Wotcher think of that! Nearly to the bone! Pretty savage baby you've brought along,' he said to William.

'I jolly well know that,' said William feelingly. 'It's your own fault for touching it. It's all right if you leave it alone. Just don't touch it, that's all. Anyway, it's mine, and I never said you could go fooling around with it, did I? It wouldn't bite *me*, I bet!'

RICHMAL CROMPTON *Just-William*, 1922, 'The Outlaws'

We found Corky near the door, looking at the picture with one hand up in a defensive sort of way, as if he thought it might swing on him . . .

'Well?' said Corky anxiously.

I hesitated a bit.

'Of course, old man, I only saw the kid once, and then only for a moment, but – but it *was* an ugly sort of kid, wasn't it, if I remember rightly?'

'As ugly as that?' . . .

'I don't see how it could have been, old chap.'

Poor old Corky ran his fingers through his hair in a temperamental sort of way. He groaned.

'You're quite right, Bertie. Something's gone wrong with the darned thing. My private impression is that, without knowing it, I've worked that stunt that Sargent used to pull – painting the soul of the sitter. I've got through the mere outward appearance, and have put the child's soul on canvas.'

'But could a child of that age have a soul like that? I don't see how he could have managed it in the time. What do you think, Jeeves?'

'I doubt it, sir.'

P. G. WODEHOUSE *Carry On, Jeeves*, 1925. ch. 2

There can be no question that Fields disliked children, in a persecuted, un-angry sort of way. His encounters with the infant thespian, Baby LeRoy, with whom he played in several films, were well known to Hollywood. He considered that the child was deliberately trying to wreck his career, and he stalked him remorselessly . . . The comedian realized that, whatever else might be going on in a scene, people would watch the antics of a baby. His competitive treatment of LeRoy was, therefore, exactly the same as he would have accorded an adult. Between takes he sat in a corner, eyed the child, and muttered vague, injured threats.

In one Fields-LeRoy picture directed by Norman Taurog, action was suspended so that the infant could have his orange juice. When the others busied themselves with scripts, Fields approached the child's nurse and said 'Why don't you take a breather? I'll give the little nipper his juice.' She nodded gratefully, and left the set.

With a solicitous nursery air, Fields shook the bottle and removed its nipple, then he drew a flask from his pocket and strengthened the citrus with a generous noggin of gin.

Baby LeRoy, a popular, warm-hearted youngster, showed his appreciation by gulping down the dynamite with a minimum of the caterwauling that distinguishes the orange-juice hour in so many homes. But when the shooting was ready to recommence, he was in a state of inoperative bliss.

Taurog and others, including the returned nurse, inspected the tot with real concern. 'I don't believe he's just sleepy,' said the nurse. 'He had a good night's rest.'

'Jiggle him some more,' suggested Taurog. 'We're running behind schedule.'

Several assistants broke into cries of 'Hold it!' 'Stand by

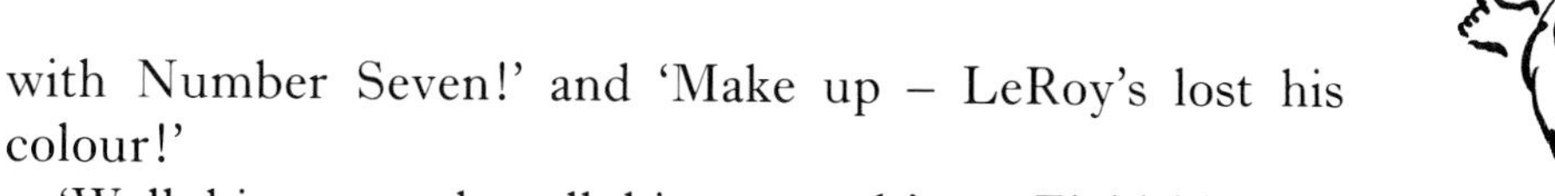

with Number Seven!' and 'Make up – LeRoy's lost his colour!'

'Walk him around, walk him around,' was Fields' hoarse and baffling comment from a secluded corner.

The child was more or less restored to consciousness, but in the scene that followed, Taurog complained of his lack of animation . . . For some inexplicable reason Fields seemed jubilant.

'He's no trouper,' he kept yelling. 'The kid's no trouper. Send him home.'

R. L. TAYLOR, *W. C. Fields*, ch. 22

L'Enfant Glacé

When Baby's cries grew hard to bear
I popped him in the Frigidaire.
I never would have done so if
I'd known that he'd be frozen stiff.
My wife said: 'George, I'm so unhappé.
Our darling's now completely frappé!'

HARRY GRAHAM *More Ruthless Rhymes*, 1930

'. . . bring in the children.'

They [the nurses] hurried out of the room and returned in a minute or two, each pushing a kind of tall dumb-waiter laden, on all its four wire-netted shelves, with eight-month-old babies, all exactly alike . . . and all (since their caste was Delta) dressed in khaki.

'Put them down on the floor.'

The infants were unloaded.

'Now turn them so that they can see the flowers and books.'

Turned, the babies at once fell silent, then began to crawl towards those clusters of sleek colours, those shapes so gay and brilliant on the white pages. As they approached, the sun came out of a momentary eclipse behind a cloud. The roses flamed up as though with a sudden passion from within; a new and profound significance seemed to suffuse the shining pages of the books. From the ranks of the crawling babies came little squeals of excitement, gurgles and twitterings of pleasure . . . The swiftest crawlers were already at their goal. Small hands reached out uncertainly, touched, grasped, unpetaling the transfigured roses, crumpling the illuminated pages of the books. The Director waited until all were happily busy. Then . . . lifting his hand, he gave the signal.

The Head Nurse, who was standing by a switchboard at the other end of the room, pressed down a little lever.

There was a violent explosion. Shriller and ever shriller, a siren shrieked. Alarm bells maddeningly sounded.

The children started, screamed; their faces were distorted with terror.

'And now,' the Director shouted (for the noise was deafen-

ing), 'now we proceed to rub in the lesson with a mild electric shock.'

He waved his hand again, and the Head Nurse pressed a second lever. The screaming of the babies suddenly changed its tone. There was something desperate, almost insane, about the sharp spasmodic yelps to which they now gave utterance. Their little bodies twitched and stiffened; their limbs moved jerkily as if to the tug of unseen wires . . .

'That's enough,' he signalled to the nurse.

The explosions ceased, the bells stopped ringing, the shriek of the siren died down from tone to tone into silence. The stiffly twitching bodies relaxed and what had become the sob and yelp of infant maniacs broadened out once more into a normal howl of ordinary terror.

'Offer them the flowers and the books again.'

The nurses obeyed; but at the approach of the roses, at the mere sight of those gaily-coloured images of pussy and cock-a-doodle-doo and baa-baa black sheep, the infants shrank away in horror; the volume of their howling suddenly increased.

'Observe,' said the Director triumphantly, 'observe.'

Books and loud noises, flowers and electric shocks – already in the infant mind these couples were compromisingly linked; and after two hundred repetitions of the same or a similar lesson would be wedded indissolubly. What man has joined, nature is powerless to put asunder.

'They'll grow up with what the psychologists used to call an "instinctive" hatred of books and flowers. Reflexes unalterably conditioned. They'll be safe from books and botany all their lives.' The Director turned to his nurses. 'Take them away again.'

Still yelling, the khaki babies were loaded on to their dumb-waiters and wheeled out, leaving behind them the smell of sour milk and a most welcome silence.

ALDOUS HUXLEY *Brave New World*, 1932, ch. 2

'. . . What does it feel like to be a mother, Sally?'

'Childbirth,' said Sally, 'is an unpleasing process. It must be quite awful for the father who, according to Walter, suffers even more than the mother. I don't quite understand about that, but of course I take his word for it. To be honest, I should like the baby a good deal better if she wasn't the split image of Walter's Aunt Lucy; all the same I am getting quite attached to her in a sort of way, and Walter's so impressed by being a father that he's actually looking out for a job. You know, motherhood is an enormous financial asset in these days; to begin with you get pounds and pounds for publishing a photograph of a child twice or three times her age and saying she's so well grown because of Gatebury's food, then you get more pounds for saying that no nursing mother would care to retire without her cup of Bovo, and finally I can now edit the Mothers' and Kiddies' Sunshine Page in the *Daily Runner* under my own name, so I get an extra pound a week for that. Oh, yes, the little dear is pulling her weight in the home and no mistake.'

NANCY MITFORD *Christmas Pudding*, 1932, ch. 3

Antonia, aged 5, when shown new baby sister:

'Do you think Gentle Jesus would care to have it back?'

In England they used to have many cases of 'overlaid' babies. Infants supposed to have been smothered when the mother rolled over them in her sleep. England regulated child life insurance, and fewer babies are 'overlaid'.

New York American, 12 December 1933

Monica and her cousin's detestable baby are in the same railway carriage as a young man-about-town, Hugo Stager, who assumes that Monica is the baby's mother. There is an accident, and the adults are concussed. Believing that they are a family, the rescuers despatch them all to Hugo's bachelor flat.

'I hope you feel better now, darling,' said the girl, bending forward and deliberately stroking Hugo's forehead. Cool, soft hands that brought infinite relief to his throbbing temples. As in a dream he caught the flash of a plain gold ring on her left hand. His eyes travelled to her face. He knew her; it was the girl in the train.

'You have had a terrible shock, dear,' she smiled tenderly.

'*Darling*,' murmured Hugo, 'it is so. I am completely off my chump. Continue the treatment, please.'

'Dada!' gurgled the baby.

'And how is the little one?' crooned Hugo.

'Baby's all right,' the girl said shortly, knitting her brows. 'An awful nuisance, as usual.'

'An awful –' Hugo sat up. 'What words are these, Harriet?'

'My name isn't Harriet. It's Monica.'

'Ah, Monica. Much better. But is this a mother's love, Monica? Do you spurn your offspring thus?'

'We'd have a much better time without it,' she pointed out frankly.

Hugo surveyed her pensively.

'So we would, Monica. In different circumstances I should escort you to the haunts of wine and song.'

She looked at him calmly. 'Why not in these circumstances?'

'Because –' retorted Hugo, in a firm voice, 'you're – dash it all!' He glowered sombrely at the brat on the hearthrug. 'I'm surprised at you, Monica!'

'We might farm it out,' she murmured.

'Goo!' said the baby, suddenly emitting sounds like a lawn-mower.

'Remove it!' cried Hugo, apprehensively, 'it's going to be sick.'

The girl rippled with unconcerned laughter and walked to the mantelpiece for a cigarette, which she lit, blowing out the smoke daintily. With a splutter the baby regained its ventral equilibrium.

Hugo wrinkled his aching forehead and strove to think this matter out. She was an undeniable peach, but there was also that undeniable wedding-ring and very concrete baby. The role of wrecker of homes did not appeal to Hugo Stager in the least. And yet – one last fling before life was to be utterly drab . . . He averted his eyes from the marbly gaze of the baby that read his guiltiest thoughts.

'Monica!'

She raised her eyebrows serenely.

'Got any glad rags with you?'

She nodded. 'My dressing-case is here.'

'Exactly. I don't know who you are, Monica, but if you

choose to drop across my path in this distinctly provocative manner you must take the consequences. Tonight we pad the hoof to Bacchanalia. In other words, Monica, you dine with me.'

She nodded again, placidly. 'I had intended to.'

Hugo frowned in perplexity. The door opened to admit the manservant bearing milk and soda.

'Binks?'

'Sir?'

'Take baby for a nice walk in the park. When you come to the pond, Binks, drop baby therein and return here. Mrs – er – Stager and I are dining out.'

Concealing his perturbation under a mask of granite, the worthy man placed the tumbler at Hugo's elbow.

'The doctor said you were to be kept quiet, sir.'

'Precisely, Binks. And how do you suppose I can be kept quiet with that baby's glassy optic fixed upon me? Remove the little one.'

The manservant shifted uneasily. The girl puffed at her cigarette with placid amusement.

'Better leave it to me,' she suggested. 'I'll dispose of it somewhere.'

'Dispose of it!' Hugo echoed. The words had a sinister sound. As if in protest the baby choked and then dribbled with lamentable freedom. Hugo shuddered.

'It ought to be put on the kerb outside a post-office,' he said, 'for people to wet their stamps on.'

The manservant tiptoed from the room in shocked silence.

SELDON TRUSS *A Century of Humour*, ed. P. G. Wodehouse, 1935, 'Hugo and the Unnatural Mother'

It is May Day. Over by the lake Mr Disraeli is walking arm-in-arm with Lord Rothschild and the Duke of Wellington.

In a nearby perambulator, kicking and gurgling, is the infant George Arliss. As the three great men approach he screws up his little face as though to impress on his memory the image of their appearance down to the smallest detail.

Mr Disraeli, Lord Rothschild and the Duke of Wellington come to a halt and gaze in silence at the infant George Arliss.

Mr Disraeli strokes his chin.

'To think,' he muses, 'that we will all three appear in the eyes of posterity looking like that.'

The Iron Duke winces.

'Don't, Mr Disraeli!' he says.

CARYL BRAHMS & S. J. SIMON *Don't, Mr Disraeli*, 1940, 'L'Envoi'

I shall never forget the kindness with which Mr and Mrs Churchill bade me farewell. He was in bed with a sore throat, and could only speak in a whisper; Mrs Churchill was sitting beside him. They told me I must have four children (as they have), and said together: 'One for Mother, one for Father, one for Accidents and one for Increase.'

ELIZABETH NEL *Mr Churchill's Secretary*, 1958, ch. 20

Babies, as all bachelors will agree, should not be allowed at large unless they are heavily draped, and fitted with various appliances for absorbing sound and moisture. If young married persons persist in their selfish pursuit of populating the planet, they should be compelled to bear the consequences. They should be shut behind high walls, clutching the terrible bundles which they have brought into the world, and when they emerge into society, if they insist on bringing these bundles with them, they should see that they are properly cloaked, muted, sealed up and, above all, *dry*. They should not wave them about in the streets to the alarm of sensitive persons who are used to the company of Siamese cats.

BEVERLEY NICHOLS *Merry Hall*, 1951, ch. 11

Gruesome Jokes

The 'sick' jokes of the early 1950s onwards ranged from the mild, and rather endearing, 'Notice seen beside the bacon cutter in a grocer's shop: "Please do not sit babies on the bacon cutter. We are getting behind with our orders"', to the Grand Guignol horror of the 'Oh Daddy' and 'Oh Mama' jokes, relished by schoolchildren and students in the late 1950s and 1960s, of which one example will suffice: 'Oh Daddy, I don't like my little brother.' 'Stop talking and get on with your dinner' (the inference being that the little brother *is* his dinner). Compared to those, the 'baby' jokes of the 1980s ('How do you keep an astronaut's baby quiet?' 'Rocket') were mildness itself.

News items from the *Sunday Pictorial*, 11 February 1951:

Married women teachers at a Cairo girls' High School were called to a conference by their director, who warned them to bring children into the world only during school holidays. Births at other times disorganised the school's work, said the director.

Mrs Jane Margaret Redden, 82, and John D. Lewis, 86, who had twenty-five children by previous marriages, told friends after their wedding in New York: 'This time we are marrying for companionship.'

A muvver was barfin' 'er biby one night,
The youngest of ten and a tiny young mite,
The muvver was poor and the biby was thin,
Only a skelington covered in skin;
The muvver turned rahnd for the soap off the rack,
She was but a moment, but when she turned back,
The biby was gorn; and in anguish she cried,
'Oh, where is my biby?' – The angels replied: –

'Your biby 'as fell dahn the plug-'ole,
Your biby 'as gorn dahn the plug;
The poor little thing was so skinny and thin
'E oughter been barfed in a jug;
Your biby is perfeckly 'appy,
'E won't need a barf any more,
Your biby 'as fell dahn the plug-'ole,
Not lorst, but gorn before.

ANON

It Must Be the Milk

There is a thought that I have tried not to but cannot help
 but think,
Which is, My goodness how much infants resemble people
 who have had too much to drink.
Tots and sots, so different and yet so identical!
What a humiliating coincidence for pride parentical!
Yet when you see your little dumpling set sail across the
 nursery floor,
Can you conscientiously deny the resemblance to somebody
 who is leaving a tavern after having tried to leave it a
 dozen times and each time turned back for just once
 more?
Each step achieved
Is simply too good to be believed;
Foot somehow follows foot
And somehow manages to stay put;
Arms wildly semaphore,
Wild eyes seem to ask, Whatever did we get in such a
 dilemma for?
And their gait is more that of a duckling than a Greek
 goddessling or godling,
And in inebriates it's called staggering but in infants it's
 called toddling.
Another kinship with topers is also by infants exhibited,
Which is that they are completely uninhibited,
And they can't talk straight
Any more than they can walk straight;
Their pronunciation is awful

And their grammar is flawful,
And in adults it's drunken and maudlin and deplorable,
But in infants it's tunnin' and adorable.
So I hope you will agree that it is very hard to tell an infant
from somebody who has gazed too long into the cup,
And really the only way you can tell them apart is to wait till
next day, and the infant is the one that feels all right
when it wakes up.

OGDEN NASH *Many Long Years Ago*, 1954

I like babies no better than I ever did. They are born far too soon. Not of course for the sailing impatient mothers-to-be, but for good taste. For the first few months they look less like human beings that precocious foetuses. The only thing to do is to look after them, since one must, but thinking hard and hopefully of grown-up schoolboys in caps. Yet we surround them with a fantastically unsuitable aura of ribbons and prettiness; lace and gossamer shawls for growing animals which thrive with almost frightening vigour in their self-made habitat of squalor. For they are quite astonishingly vigorous, and certainly need to be to survive the varying and contradictory fashions of baby-care.

NAN FAIRBROTHER *Children in the House*, 1954

William, his breakfast over, was very quickly aware of some disturbance in his usual morning routine, and was not long in announcing his displeasure.

'Out-door! *Out-door!*' he protested when it became increasingly clear his mother was going about her usual business, but without installing him in his playpen in the back yard, where every fine morning, side by side with the hens crooning in their soap box, crooning back in return, he grubbed in the dust with an old kitchen spoon or murmured endearments to a small wooden horse very much the worse for wear.

'Not today, my lovey,' said Mrs Ruggles for the twentieth time, 'not today. No, I *know* it's not raining' – as a loud yell pealed forth – '*but you can't go out!*' . . .

'Out-door! Out-door!' wailed William, banging on the table with a spoon. 'Out-*door*!' And suddenly, furious with frustration, he seized a tea-cup and flung it on the floor where it broke into half a dozen pieces. He then let forth one of the loudest of his famous yells.

Rarely Mrs Ruggles lost her temper with him; more rarely still would she acknowledge he was spoilt. Now, suddenly, she did both.

'Stop making that noise – *at once*!' she cried, running in from the back kitchen and giving him a little shake and pointing to the smashed cup. 'You're a naughty, spoilt boy! Stop it! Do you hear? *Stop it!*' And then, as William only yelled the louder, she picked up the remains of the cup, put it on the table, and smartly smacked both his hands. 'Naughty, spoilt boy!' she repeated.

For a second, from sheer surprise, William remained silent; then he opened his mouth and *roared*.

There were few tears – the smacks had not been hard ones; he roared only with outraged dignity, and fury.

'Be *quiet*!' cried Mrs Ruggles, shouting to make herself heard above the din, '*at once!*' But William only roared louder.

Really this couldn't go on; next thing the neighbours 'ud be in to know what was up . . .

Mrs Ruggles went quickly into the back kitchen. The next minute she returned with his push-chair; picked him up, dumped him into it, fastened him in securely with the straps, and giving his chair a little shake, pushed it into the middle of the room.

'Now stop it!' she cried, '*or up you go to your cot!*' And taking no further notice of him, she collected the breakfast things off the table, carried them into the back kitchen, and set about the washing-up.

For another two or three minutes William howled lustily, kicked, and banged on the sides of his push-chair with his fists, but all to no avail. He remained alone.

Mrs Ruggles finished the washing-up. The noise was subsiding somewhat; by the time she had peeled the potatoes, sorted out the washing, and lit the boiler, there was only an occasional plaintive sniff from the kitchen. A few minutes later, no sound at all. She peeped round the door. Worn out with defeat and tears, William slept.

EVE GARNETT *Further Adventures of the Family from One End Street*, 1956, ch. 9

Child Talk

Any brothers or sisters?
I have a brother one week old.
What can he do?
He can say 'Mamma' and 'Daddy'.
Can he walk?
No, he's too lazy.

Any brothers and sisters?
A two months old brother.
How does he behave?
He cries all night.
Why is that, do you think?
He probably thinks he's missing something on television.

What do you want to be?
A nurse in a maternity hospital.
Who gave you that idea?
Nobody. I just like babies.
What would you do with a screaming, whimpering, crying, kicking baby?
That's easy; I'd leave it alone.

'Well,' said the friendly neighbour, 'I hear you've got a little baby brother at your house. What do you think of him?'

'I don't like him,' said Sally frankly. 'He's got a funny red face and he cries all the time.'

'Why don't you send him back where he came from?'

'Oh, I'm afraid we couldn't do that. We've used him two days already.'

Professor Todlipp's Love-child

Professor Todlipp had no Wife
In all the Ups and Downs of Life,
Avoided Matrimonial Strife
By living with an Only Sister
In a villa 'Bella Vista'
Sexless as the Aspidistra.

The Professor's softest cardiac spot
Lay not with Blonde or Hottentot,
But with frogs – amphibious lot:
Frogs that hopped and frogs that climbed,
Frogs that croaked and frogs that chimed,
Frogs unclassified, unrhymed.

There came by Air Mail one bluff day
From the green steams of Paraguay
Unfertilized frogspawn in a tray.
Professor Todlipp deaf (and dumb)
To any sense of what might come
Took a needle, pricked his thumb.

With that needle, now lymphatic,
Advanced upon the tray, ecstatic,
Pricked the spawn in gesture Attic,
Then turning to his Only Sister
Remarked as soberly he kissed her
'Observe, my dear, that little Blister.'

That little blister quickly grew
A head, a tail, and features too
'Now here's a Merry How d'ye do,'
remarked Miss Todlipp, limp with shame
(And that Blister soon became
A Blot upon the Family Name!).

A tadpole first it swam apace
But oh! Sad Omen of Disgrace
Above the tail poor Todlipp's face!
And when the frogling left its jar
And hopped across the Axminster
It hailed them each as 'Ma' and 'Pa'.

SHAMUS FRAZER *Yet More Comic & Curious Verse*,
ed. Cohen, 1959, verses 3, 5–9

Margaret was always having to remind Arthur and Charles to make less noise, though there was nothing she could do about Edgar, who lay in the bassinet and cried angrily all day long.

'You'd think he would get tired,' said Arthur, peering into the Moses' basket one afternoon as they had just dragged up the stairs back from their walk. 'But he just goes on, hour after hour, and he doesn't seem to mind it at all. I think he's louder now than when we went out for the walk. I wish I could make a noise like that.'

GILLIAN AVERY *To Tame a Sister*, 1961, ch. 1

(New York, Thursday) A premature 5lb baby girl was critically ill with lead poisoning today after swallowing before birth a bullet fired by an unknown attacker at her mother . . . Police said the mother, 20-year-old Mrs Lucy Ortiz, who was eight months pregnant, was standing at the open window of her apartment at about 1 a.m. on Tuesday morning. The attacker fired and his .22 bullet entered the right side of her stomach. She was rushed to King's County Hospital where an emergency Caesarean operation was performed. Doctors were unable to find the bullet, but when they X-rayed the child were astonished to find the bullet lodged in its stomach. They said the child apparently swallowed the bullet, which caused the lead poisoning.

Daily Express, 14 June 1968

Dirk, aged 12, is faced with a newborn brother, after an eleven-year gap:

It was Nurse Hennessy, at the top of the stairs, who called me . . . She was smiling and carried a white bundle.

'Come up and meet your little brother!' she cried as if we were at a party.

It looked, from my point of view, like rabbit-offal wrapped in a shawl. I was silent with shock at the sight of this living stranger in our midst. This was the bulge in my mother's belly. This was the cause of the vastly disturbed household . . . She unwrapped the offal and laid it in my reluctant arms.

'Hold its neck. Otherwise its head will fall off, and we don't want that, do we!' I was not altogether sure . . .

From somewhere far away it seemed we heard the first cries. Angry, defiant, furious at being late . . . The crying went on. It was not to stop for two years . . . I knew, with savage insight, that I detested that screaming bundle of waving arms and legs on the floor below . . . a mounting wave of dislike and anger rose within me which nearly made me sick. I would never forgive that stinking, smelly, shrieking little beast who had burst, unwelcome, into my perfect Two Pivot and Centre Life. And I didn't for over twenty years.

DIRK BOGARDE *A Postillion Struck by Lightning*, 1977, ch. 9

They all had small children. And they were all married to men who thought of their lives in terms of career, not job . . . They didn't bother much about their clothes: they always had children's sticky hands all over them, or the sour milk of babies' spit-up. Conversation was a physical challenge, words uttered while a baby clung to a neck or sat on a lap tugging Mother's ear, or while leaping up to get to Johnny before he swallowed that stone, to get to Midge before she clobbered Johnny over the head with that shovel, or to pull Deena out from the little space in the fence where she'd wedged herself trying to escape from the yard.

For all its activity, it was a lazy life because it went nowhere. One day was like another: the sun shone or it did not; jackets were needed, or heavy snowsuits and boots. Toilet training proceeded or snagged. Sometimes the sheets froze on the clotheslines. The women worked in the mornings, the late afternoons, and sometimes in the evenings, when they would mend or iron or sew a new outfit for Cheryl or Midge while the TV set blared 'Dragnet' or Mike Wallace. It was not a bad life; it was a hell of a lot better than collecting coins at a toll booth all day, or examining cans as they came off the assembly line. The unspoken, unthought-about conditions that made it oppressive had long since been accepted by all of them: that they had not chosen but had been automatically slotted into their lives, and that they were never free to move (the children were much more effective as clogs than confinement on a prison farm would be). Having accepted the shit and string beans, they were content.

MARILYN FRENCH *The Women's Room*, 1977,
pt. 2, ch. 5

A tale from Minneapolis should interest parents whose children are prone to bouts of ear-splitting screams. One mother complained that she had been made temporarily deaf by the yells of her 11-month-old baby. A couple of scientists, intrigued by the possibility, measured the volume of the screams about 15 cm from the child – to simulate the distance from the source of the yells to the mother's ear. Their astonishing discovery was that the child could produce a scream about 30 times louder than normal conversation and the volume – when the baby was at full throttle – was almost comparable with a pneumatic drill. The child's screams ranged from 100 to 117 decibels with an average of 108.

The Times, 6 Jan. 1984, reporting from the *New England Journal of Medicine*

Unpublished Opinions

Woman in train, c. *65*
Oh, here's a baby coming in – I'll move to another carriage. I always do. It's the crying that gets me. It's so relentless. It must be something wrong with our culture, actually, because they don't cry like that in Africa.

Aunt, aged 60
I looked sadly at my great-nephews and thought how much easier it would have been if they'd been kittens, because then they would have liked me and I would have liked them. They were the most unprepossessing babies.

Woman television broadcaster, aged 43
I hate babies. I'd be terrified if someone gave me one to hold. I hate them squawling in supermarkets. I feel I'd like to run them over with the supermarket trolley.

When my first son was born in 1944 he had reddish tints in his hair and I enquired, in passing, of my mother whether there was any history of red hair in our family. 'Oh yes,' she replied, 'Our Charlie had red hair'. When I asked who on earth our Charlie was, since I had never heard of him before, she said, 'No dear, he was one of my younger brothers but he was drowned when he was about eighteen months old.' 'Oh Mum,' I sympathised, 'what a dreadful tragedy. How on earth did it happen?' 'Well dear,' she said, 'It was my fault, I took him down to the harbour one day and forgot to put the brake on the pram. While I was playing a man called out, "Eh, Missee, is that your pram?", and I turned round and there was the pram with our Charlie in it rushing down the slipway into the sea.' 'Oh my God,' I said, 'It must have haunted you ever since. Is that why you never talk about it?' 'Not really,' she said, 'I was upset about it at the time but looking back I realise that it was probably an act of God because there were far too many mouths in our family to feed', and then she added as an afterthought, 'But it was a pity about the pram. It was a good pram and we could have done with that'. I was absolutely rivetted to the spot in horror and disbelief that *my* mother, this gentle little lady who had given so much loving care to my brother and me and in fact to any children with whom she had close contact, could ever have voiced such terrible sentiments. My horror was first directed against her, but afterwards against the kind of society which induced the poor to accept such a wholly unacceptable and frightening philosophy. And people sometimes ask me why I am a socialist!

'Our Olive': The Autobiography of Olive Gibbs, 1989, ch. 1

Notes

p. 4 Lucian of Samosata's fantasy may come true, for we are now told that the womb is not the only place where an embryo may be harboured until ready for birth – any corner of the human body will do, whether female or male.

p. 9 *The Diary of Samuel Pepys*, ed. R. Latham & W. Matthews, IV, 37, 48.

p. 12 The full title of this bitterly satirical pamphlet is: *A Modest Proposal for preventing the children of poor people from becoming a burthen to their parents or country, and for making them beneficial to the publick*.

p. 14 Whoever wrote this exhausting documentary of life with a baby – and it has long been attributed to Jonathan Swift – used the traditional dandling song 'Hey! my kitten, a kitten' as his starting point (see *The Oxford Dictionary of Nursery Rhymes*, no. 288).

p. 17 'O that I had ne'er been married.' First recorded *c.* 1770. See *Songs from David Herd's Manuscripts*, ed. Hans Hecht, 1904, p. 112.

p. 18 *Boswell: The Ominous Years, 1774–1776*, ed. C. Ryskamp & F. A. Pottle, 1963.

p. 18 *Thraliana. The Diary of Mrs H. L. Thrale*, ed. K. C. Balderston, I, 1942, p. 12.

p. 22 This joke has been told of many couples – perhaps most memorably of the actress Mrs Patrick Campbell and

George Bernard Shaw. 'Mrs Pat' was said to have suggested that between them they might produce a perfect human being, and GBS to have retorted that ten to one the child would inherit his looks and her brains.

p. 23 'O can ye sew cushions?' This traditional nursing song was submitted to John Johnson, for his *Musical Museum*, by Robert Burns.

p. 25 'Needles and pins.' The second couplet, previously unrecorded, came from a ten-year-old boy in Maud, Aberdeenshire, 1975.

p. 29 A writer in *Notes & Queries* remembered hearing some of the verses in 1836, and it seems reasonable to suppose that this version was known in Napoleon Bonaparte's day.

p. 34 'A Serenade', line 22. Poppy-syrup had for centuries brought relief to tired parents. Paelo Bagellardo said, in his *Book on Infant Diseases*, 1472, 'our common people give infants a little of the stuff called "Quietness"'; this was an extract of black poppies or poppy seeds, and was, of course, a form of opium. During the nineteenth century doctors increasingly warned against the use of opiates; as Dr Thomas Bull stated in *Hints to Mothers*, 2nd edn, 1839, 'they are but too often fatal to the little patients'.

p. 37 'Willie Winkie.' Miller's 'Willie Winkie' was printed in the third series of *Whistle-Binkie: a collection of comic and sentimental songs, chiefly original*, published by David Robertson in Glasgow, 1841. Robertson had been doubtful about accepting the song, but it was immediately and immensely successful. No trace has been found of the nursery rhyme 'Wee Willie Winkie' before 1841, but it is possible that it was already known, and that Miller used it as the basis of his poem.

p. 45 *Dearest Child: Letters between Queen Victoria and the Princess Royal 1858–1861*, ed. Roger Fulford, 1964, p. 191.

p. 52 'Aboriginal Poems for Infant Minds.' Three of the rhymes which were, in *Punch*, 30 March 1861, attributed to 'Lord Macaulay's New Zealander' (he who Macaulay envisaged, in his essay on Ranke's *History of the Popes*, as standing in some future time 'on a broken arch of London Bridge to sketch the ruins of St Paul's'). The author was Charles W. Brooks ('Shirley Brooks'), *Punch*'s editor. His title parodies Ann and Jane Taylor's *Original Poems for Infant Minds*. The third of the 'poems' given here mimics 'What! cry when I wash you, not love to be clean!' from their *Rhymes for the Nursery*; and the second 'poem' is of course a parody of 'Pat-a-cake, pat-a-cake, baker's man'.

p. 54 'If you rock an empty cradle.' This is one of the frequent contributions from Chambers' correspondent 'C. W. J.' of Suffolk, who seems to take a less sympathetic than scientific interest in the poor 'mother of ten'.

p. 55 'The Royal Baby.' Music-hall song written by C. H. Witt, Esq., and sung by 'The Great Vance' soon after the birth of Prince Albert Victor on 8 January 1864. Prince Albert was the Prince of Wales's eldest son. He died in 1892, leaving his brother to inherit the throne as George V.

p. 72 'Under This sOd.' From *The Bradford Observer*, 14 October 1876, p. 5.

p. 74 'Mrs Winslow's Soothing Syrup.' This song, like 'A Serenade' (p. 34), is in praise of opiates, the most famous form of which for babies was Mother Siegel's Soothing Syrup. Composed by Alfred Lee, with words by W. R. Gordon, the song seems to have been very popular in its day. In the year following its publication Elgar wrote a wind quintet with the same title – 'Mrs Winslow's

Soothing Syrup' – but there is no musical connection between the two pieces.

p. 80 'My Baby.' Slightly edited from *The Swim Out for Glory Songster, containing all the latest negro songs, etc.*, 1882.

p. 88 'Oh! let me kiss the baby.' From 'Folklore of Grant County, Indiana, in the Nineties', W. L. McAtee, *Midwest Folklore*, Winter 1951, p. 253.

p. 94 'Holly-o, mistletoe.' A rhyme that belongs to the days when the eldest girl of the family was put in charge of the baby. This particular version is from Mark Benney's *11th Contact Book*, 1948, and was known in the East End of London *c.* 1918 ('Holly O, Mistletoe!' was an old London street cry, see *London Cries*, A. W. Tuer, 1885). In other places, for instance in Hull in the 1890s, the rhyme began 'Eenie, meenie, miney, mo'.

p. 95 'Fudge, fudge.' This rhyme has been used for jumping rope in America since at least the 1930s. It came over to Britain in the late 1940s.

p. 96 'Over the garden wall.' Popular with schoolchildren from at least as early as 1905, for ball-bouncing, or skipping, or just chanting. It is possibly an irreverent child-version of the sentimental song 'Over the Garden Wall' of *c.*1880, of which the chorus is:

Over the garden wall,
The sweetest girl of all,
There never was yet such eyes of jet,
And you may bet I'll never forget
The night our lips in kisses met,
Over the garden wall.

p. 96 'Miss Susie had a baby.' An amalgamation of two American rhymes which go back to the 1920s, this is one of the most popular hand-clapping games of the present day,

and is typical of the schoolchild's off-hand attitude towards babies. This version is from Connecticut, 1977. The mysterious 'lady with the alligator purse' is the old-time midwife. In Betty Smith's *A Tree Grows in Brooklyn* when the midwife is called she grabs 'her crocodile satchel – familiar to everyone in the neighbourhood and believed by all the youngsters to be the satchel in which they had been delivered, kicking, to their mothers.'

p. 98 'The Grizzly Bear.' The original version, which must have had an illustration, ran:

> Reader, behold! this monster wild
> Has gobbled up the infant child, etc.

It appears among 'Light Verse and Parodies written at various times between 1887 and 1927' in *A. E. H. Some Poems, Some Letters and a Personal Memoir by his Brother Laurence Housman*, 1937, p. 236.

p. 100 'Johnnie in the Cradle.' School of Scottish Studies. Adapted from the tale collected by Hamish Henderson in 1955 from Andrew Stewart, Blairgowrie, who learnt it from his mother.

p. 114 *Don't, Mr Disraeli*. George Arliss was the great, but personally not very prepossessing, actor who played the title-role in the play *Disraeli* (1911; afterwards made into a film), Lord Rothschild in the film *The House of Rothschild*, and the Duke of Wellington in the film (his first in Britain) *The Iron Duke*.

p. 116 'A muvver was barfin' 'er biby.' From *Verse and Worse*, Arnold Silcock, 1952.

p. 122 'Child Talk.' Three dialogues from Art Linkletter's *Kids Say the Darndest Things*, 1957, selected from the CBS television and radio show in which he chatted with children from the Los Angeles neighbourhood; and a vintage 'kid story' from the same book.

Acknowledgements

We owe a special debt of gratitude to Miss Damaris Hayman, whose breadth of reading and phenomenal memory have greatly enriched this book.

We would also like to thank the following for permission to include copyright material:

Gillian Avery, *To Tame A Sister*, London 1961. Reprinted by permission of Gillian Avery; Dirk Bogarde, *A Postillion Struck by Lightning*, London 1977. Reprinted by permission of the author and Chatto & Windus; James Boswell, *Journal* from *Boswell: The Ominous Years*, ed. Charles Ryskamp and Frederick A. Pottle, New York 1963. Copyright © Yale University; Caryl Brahms and S. J. Simon, *Don't, Mr Disraeli*, London 1940. Reprinted by permission of Mr Ned Sherrin; Richmal Crompton, *Just William*, London 1922. Reprinted by permission of Pan/Macmillan Children's Books; Nan Fairbrother, *Children in the House*, London 1954. Reprinted by permission of the estate of the author and Chatto & Windus; Shamus Frazer, *Professor Todlipp's Love Child*, from *Yet More Comic and Curious Verse* edited by J. M. Cohen. Reprinted by permission of Shamus Frazer; Marilyn French, *The Women's Room*, New York 1977. Reprinted by permission of the author; Eve Garnett, *Further Adventures of the Family from One End Street*, London 1956. Reprinted by permission of Heinemann Young Books; Olive Gibbs, *'Our Olive': The Autobiography of Olive Gibbs*, Oxford

1989. Reprinted by permission of Robert Dugdale; Robert Graves and Raphael Patai, *Hebrew Myths: The Book of Genesis*, London 1963. Reprinted by kind permission of A. P. Watt Limited on behalf of the trustees of the Robert Graves Copyright Trust and Raphael Patai; Aldous Huxley, *Leda*, London 1920, and *Brave New World*, London 1932. Reprinted by permission of Mrs Laura Huxley and Chatto & Windus; Art Linkletter, *Kids Say the Darndest Things*, 1957. Reprinted by permission of Prentice Hall; Lucian of Samosata, *True History*, London 1958. Translated by Paul Turner and reprinted by permission of John Calder (Publishers) Limited; Nancy Mitford, *Christmas Pudding*, London 1932. Reprinted by permission of the Peters Fraser & Dunlop Group Limited; Thomas More, *Utopia*, London 1961. Translated by Paul Turner and reprinted by permission of Penguin Books Limited; Ogden Nash, *Many Long Years Ago*, London 1954. Reprinted by permission of Curtis Brown Limited; Elizabeth Nel, *Mr Churchill's Secretary*, London 1958. Reprinted by permission of Hodder and Stoughton Limited; Beverley Nichols, *Merry Hall*, London 1951. Reprinted by permission of Eric Glass Ltd and Jonathan Cape; His Honour Judge Parry, *The First Book of Krabb*, 1897, and *The Scarlet Herring*, 1899. Reprinted by permission of Christy & Moore and Anthony Sheil Associates Ltd; Samuel Pepys, *The Diary of Samuel Pepys 1662*, London 1971. Edited by R. Latham and W. Matthews and reproduced by kind permission of Unwin Hyman Ltd; W. H. D. Rouse, *Gods, Heroes and Men of Ancient Greece*, London 1934. Reproduced by permission of The Master and Fellows of Christ's College, Cambridge; Hester Lynch Thrale, *Thralania: The Diary of Mrs Hester Lynch Thrale*, London 1951. Edited by Katharine C. Balderston and reproduced by kind permission of Oxford University Press; Queen Victoria, Letter to the Princess Royal, 4 May 1859, from *Dearest Child: Letters between Queen Victoria and the Princess Royal 1858–1861*, London 1964. Edited by Roger Fulford and reproduced by kind permission of the Royal Archives; P. G. Wodehouse, *Carry On Jeeves*, London 1925. Reprinted by permission of Random

Century Group and A. P. Watt Ltd on behalf of the trustees of the Wodehouse Trust No. 3.

While every effort has been made to secure permission, we may have failed in a few cases to trace the copyright holder. We apologize for any apparent negligence.

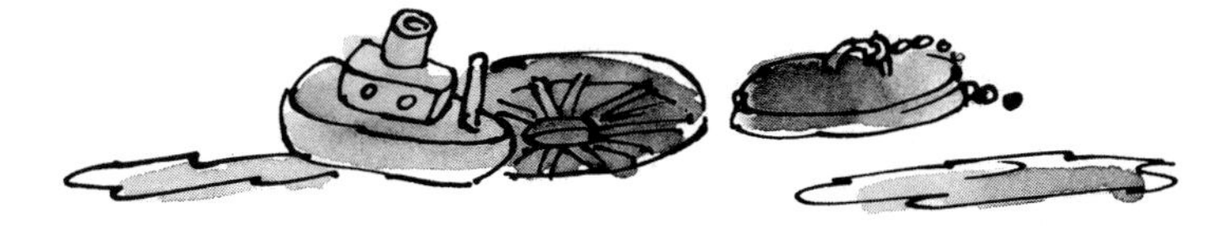

Index to Authors